Great Places in America:
Great Streets and Neighborhoods, 2007 Designees

Introduction 1

Great Streets

Chapter 1. 125th Street, Harlem, New York 2

Chapter 2. Bull Street, Savannah, Georgia 6

Chapter 3. Canyon Road, Santa Fe, New Mexico 10

Chapter 4. Delmar Loop, University City and St. Louis, Missouri 14

Chapter 5. Main Street, Northampton, Massachusetts 18

Chapter 6. Monument Avenue, Richmond, Virginia 22

Chapter 7. North Michigan Avenue, Chicago, Illinois 26

Chapter 8. Ocean Drive, Miami, Florida 30

Chapter 9. South Temple Street, Salt Lake City, Utah 34

Chapter 10. St. Charles Avenue, New Orleans, Louisiana 38

Great Neighborhoods

Chapter 11. **Chatham Village, Pittsburgh, Pennsylvania** 42

Chapter 12. **Eastern Market, Washington, D.C.** 46

Chapter 13. **Elmwood Village, Buffalo, New York** 50

Chapter 14. **First Addition, Lake Oswego, Oregon** 54

Chapter 15. **Hillcrest, San Diego, California** 58

Chapter 16. **North Beach, San Francisco, California** 62

Chapter 17. **Old West Austin, Austin, Texas** 66

Chapter 18. **Park Slope, Brooklyn, New York** 70

Chapter 19. **Pike Place Market, Seattle, Washington** 74

Chapter 20. **West Urbana, Urbana, Illinois** 78

Introduction

Great places are all around us—in small towns and big cities, suburbs and metropolitan areas scattered throughout the country from East to West and North to South. We live, work, visit, and recreate in great places. From time to time, we may stop and ask, What makes this place great?

In endeavoring to celebrate excellence in planning and the unique elements and important attributes of exceptional places, the American Planning Association (APA) launched the annual *Great Places in America* program in April 2007. This report provides a snapshot of the first 20 designations--10 neighborhoods and 10 streets—which were announced October 2, 2007, in Washington, D.C., during National Community Planning Month. Starting in 2008, APA is adding a third category of designations, Great Public Spaces, which will involve 10 such places being recognized each year.

The neighborhoods and streets designated in 2007 stand out as places of exceptional character and lasting value. They are memorable, perhaps even famous, but each deeply cared for and valued. *Great Places in America* seeks to recognize areas that not only visitors find appealing, but that are enjoyed and appreciated by those who work and live there everyday.

Great Places in America considers a wide range of criteria, including affordability; accessibility and equality; environmental stewardship and sustainability; urban and architectural design; and safety. Also considered is a place's history, amenities, architecture and design, sustainability, civic engagement and participation, geography, diversity, affordability, and socioeconomic factors.

Other important characteristics of these places include a legacy of planning, cultural and historical assets, attractiveness to people, and a sustainable approach to the future. Through the Great Places program, APA also seeks to recognize streets, neighborhoods, and public spaces that accommodate the needs of culturally, socially, and economically diverse groups of people.

In addition, *Great Places in America* presents a distinctive approach to singling out communities with a strong local identity and sense of place that reflects their own unique past, present, and future. Designated places underscore the valuable contributions planners and planning play in helping create outstanding neighborhoods, streets, and public spaces.

Great places do not just happen or come about on their own. It takes leadership and community involvement from all involved—the mayor and other elected officials, the business and investment communities, and residents and neighborhood organizations. It is the accumulation of millions of individual decisions made by these groups of people and others—sometimes big, sometimes small—that continue to influence the quality of these places. When putting everything together—a commitment to planning, strong local identity, historical assets, a place that people find safe and friendly, and a sustainable approach to the future—the result is a great place.

The great places described in this PAS Report represent the first of many shining lights communities can follow—examples of strong, healthy places where people care about where they live, work, and play. We congratulate the elected officials, community and business leaders, engaged citizens, and planners who joined together to create these exceptional places. APA looks forward to recognizing and celebrating many more great places in years to come and encourages you to suggest places you think should be considered by completing the online form located at www.planning.org/greatplaces.

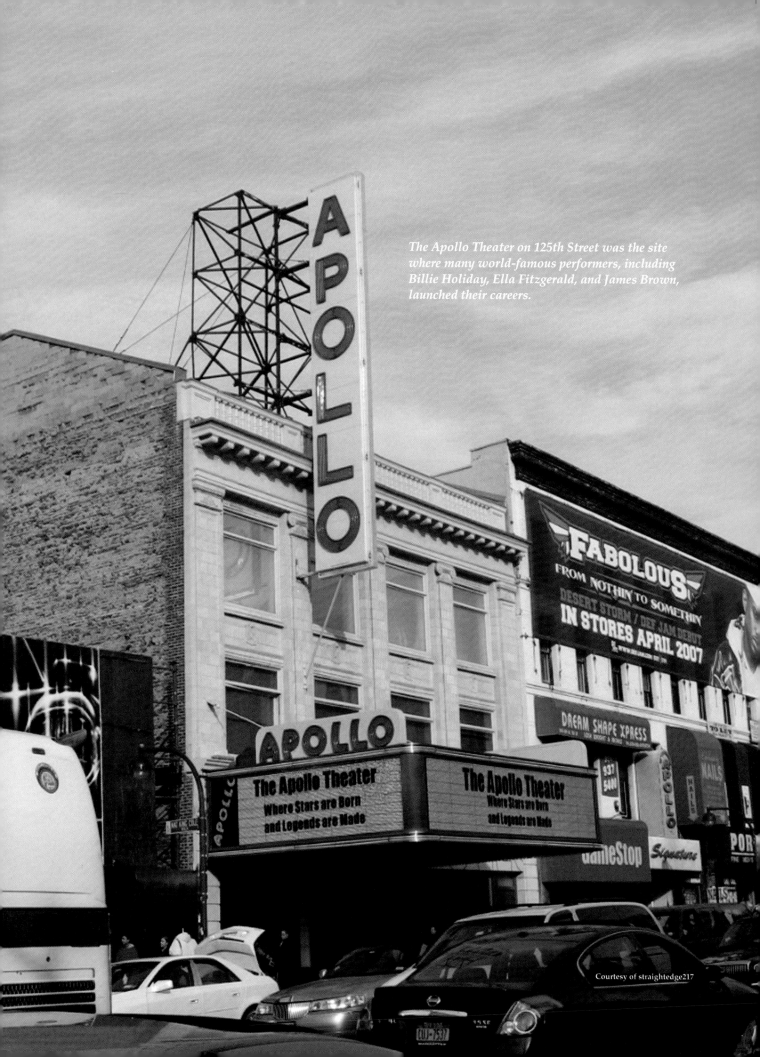

The Apollo Theater on 125th Street was the site where many world-famous performers, including Billie Holiday, Ella Fitzgerald, and James Brown, launched their careers.

CHAPTER 1

125th Street
Harlem, New York

Despite decades of tremendous population growth, strained infrastructure, disinvestment, and urban renewal, 125th Street in Harlem has managed to maintain its identity as the country's capital of African-American culture.

Locally renowned and internationally celebrated, Manhattan's 125th Street has long been Harlem's "Main Street." It is not just a regional business corridor; it is also a local retail destination. Despite handling large amounts of vehicular traffic, the 1.75-mile street is a favorite of pedestrians who use it to access public transportation, both bus and subway, and for shopping.

A broad array of architecture is found here, including early single-family brownstones, tenement apartments, warehouses, Art Deco commercial structures, early office buildings, and midcentury modern buildings. Most buildings are low in scale, which helps the street avoid the "canyon" effect found in midtown Manhattan.

Transportation, more than any other single factor, influenced Harlem's development. . . .
Harlem became Manhattan's first suburb and was considered one of its most
fashionable residential neighborhoods.

Some 83,000 African-Americans
called Harlem home in the 1920s,
a number that grew to 200,000 by
1930.

This wall mural at the corner of 125th
Street and Lenox Avenue is just one
example of the many ways the street
enlivens its public space.

First conceived in the 1811 Commissioner's Plan of New York City, which created the city's famous grid, 125th Street is one of 15 broad, crosstown streets that occur at regular intervals—roughly every 10 blocks. Perhaps more than the other 14 major east-west connectors, 125th Street was best positioned for intensive use due to both the island's topography and its development. The next broad street to the north, 135th, tapers dramatically due to the sweep of the Harlem River to the east and St. Nicholas Park to the west. To the south, 116th Street is broken up by Columbia University and Morningside Park. As the roadway connecting the Triborough Bridge, FDR Drive, and the Henry Hudson Parkway, 125th Street is a natural route for private and commercial vehicles traveling within the city, to the outer boroughs, or to points beyond.

Transportation, more than any other single factor, influenced Harlem's development. With the 1835 opening of the New York and Harlem Railroad, which ran along Park Avenue from City Hall to the Harlem River, Harlem became Manhattan's first suburb and was considered one of its most fashionable residential neighborhoods.

While black farmers had settled in Harlem as early as 1830, it wasn't until the 1920s that the African-American population soared. Some 83,000 black residents called Harlem home in 1920. Ten years later, the number surpassed 200,000. The Harlem Renaissance was underway, and 125th Street was the epicenter of the black cultural experience. The world-famous Apollo Theater on 125th helped launch the careers of such prominent entertainers as Billie Holiday, Ella Fitzgerald, James Brown, Stevie Wonder, and Aretha Franklin.

The Great Depression brought new construction and building maintenance to a halt. Thriving neighborhoods deteriorated into slums. The Works Progress Administration built the Harlem River Houses, 557 units of low-rise public housing, the first such housing in Harlem and, today, one of the best maintained.

After World War II, the street and its surrounding neighborhoods continued to decline, even as the Federal Housing Act fueled urban renewal and slum redevelopment in major cities throughout the U.S. Although a limited amount of "superblock" housing was constructed along 125th Street during this period, other nearby urban renewal redevelopment projects contributed to the destruction of historic Harlem housing and exacerbated disinvestment in the area.

The 1990s brought renewed interest in the revitalization of 125th Street. The Apollo Theater underwent a $20 million renovation that added a state-of-the art entertainment complex, a recording studio, and a television production center. Harlem USA, a $66 million

In 2007, city planners put forward a comprehensive rezoning of 125th Street to encourage its development as a regional business corridor by stimulating new investment and new cultural and retail activities.

retail and entertainment complex held its grand opening in 2000. The 285,000-square-foot development included a nine-screen theater and major franchises, such as Old Navy and The Disney Store. More recently, construction commenced on a 21-story, 600,000-square-foot office complex, Harlem Park, at 125th Street and Park Avenue. The striking glass tower, slated to open in 2009, is being built to the Silver certification standard of the Leadership in Energy and Environmental Design (LEED) Green Building Rating System™ and will include 82,000 square feet of retail.

This and other new activity have led the New York City Department of City Planning to undertake an extensive review of Harlem's "Main Street" to assess its current and future role. In October 2007, city planners put forward for public review a comprehensive rezoning of 125th Street to encourage its development as a regional business corridor by stimulating new investment as well as new cultural and retail activities. The proposals include creation of an arts and entertainment district that would encompass existing institutions, including the Apollo Theater and Studio Museum. Other zoning changes would improve the pedestrian experience by ensuring that active uses occupy the ground floor of new developments.

Complementing the city's new zoning proposals is an approved street lighting and lamppost project being pursued by the 125th Street Business Improvement District. Meanwhile, the Harlem Community Development Corporation is working with the New York State Office of General Services to redesign the plaza in front of the Adam Clayton Powell, Jr., State Office Building. Shade trees will be added as a buffer between the street and plaza that hosts a farmer's market and provides residents convenient access to fresh, regional produce during the summer.

On the west end of 125th Street, another revitalization program is underway. The $19 million West Harlem Piers project will turn a city-owned parking lot into an attractive and accessible waterfront amenity. The piers will support fishing, water tours, boating, and ecological exploration, among other activities. A variety of vessels, including excursion boats and water taxis, will be able to dock at West Harlem. A bicycle and pedestrian path will provide a critical link in the waterfront greenway, connecting Cherry Walk on the southern end of the site with the northern segment of Riverside Park.

As change comes to 125th Street, the community—including residents and businesses—is working closely with planners and local officials to ensure that the physical and social environments continue to embrace those who choose to live, work, and shop on this truly unique street.

Even with a substantial change in character and scale on 125th St. in the 1990s, small stores, like this local hardware and garden shop, still prove popular along this great street.

The square across from the Adam Clayton Powell, Jr., State Office Building is home to a farmer's market. It is destined for a redesign, including the addition of shade trees for shoppers and merchants, to serve as a buffer between the building's plaza and the market.

Bull Street benefits from its urban tree canopy and elegant home entrances along with a variety of architecture, public buildings, public squares, and houses of worship for a number of denominations.

CHAPTER 2

Bull Street
Savannah, Georgia

Cars, pedestrians, bikes, skateboards, carriages, and trolleys amicably share space along the 10-block stretch of Bull Street that begins at City Hall and ends at Forsyth Park. But walk those same blocks and the feeling is that of a more relaxed era. As Savannah celebrates the 275th anniversary of the plan that gave birth to this mixed-use corridor, the heart of the city's downtown bustles with history and activity. It has stood the test of time.

Bull Street is in the center of a National Historic Landmark District, one of the largest in the United States. Savannah features 24 public squares. Four of Bull Street's squares were included by General James Edward Oglethorpe in his 1733 plan for the city. In this unusual orthogonal plan, streets and building lots are arranged around a central open space. The repetitive street grid connects one neighborhood to another and one public square to the next. Between the Revolutionary and Civil Wars, Savannah and Bull Street continued to develop according to Oglethorpe's plan.

Known as The Forest City, Savannah began the strategic planting of trees along streets and boulevards and in parks and squares in 1891.

Johnson Square, one of four squares on Bull Street and 24 in Savannah, was included in the 1733 plan for the city.

The historic Savannah Theater, built in 1818, as seen from Chippewa Square.

Each of Bull Street's five squares can be approached from eight public rights of way—one each from the north and south, and three each from the east and west. As all vehicles must circumvent the squares, traffic flows at a leisurely pace. While the streets are heavily used, the intersections around the squares lack stoplights.

Planted mostly in live oaks, which form lovely canopies, the squares feature wide brick sidewalks and welcoming benches. Some contain fountains or public art. Originally used for military purposes, many of the squares are adorned with statues commemorating the city's history. Bull Street's Chippewa Square, for instance, was laid out in 1815 and named for a battle in the War of 1812. The square, featured in the movie *Forrest Gump*, hosts a bronze and marble monument to Oglethorpe. Today, the street's squares may be rented for special events and private functions.

Bull Street and its squares serve as a living studio of sorts for the 6,000 students at the Savannah College of Art and Design. For nearly three decades, the school has made the city its campus, investing millions of dollars renovating and restoring some 60 buildings. Its admissions office and Rapid Transit Gallery, which showcases graduate student thesis works, are at 342 Bull Street.

Known as The Forest City, Savannah began the strategic planting of trees along streets and boulevards and in parks and squares in 1891. Five years later, the Park and Tree Commission was created to ensure the orderly forestation and beautification of the city. Recognizing that much of Savannah's charm is owed to its urban forest, the city plants more than 1,000 new trees each year. In the downtown and Victorian districts, efforts are underway to remove sidewalk pavement to create additional spaces for plantings.

As those first trees were being planted, the paving of Bull Street began. Late in 1891, the city's mayor, John J. McDonough, noted in his annual report, "The citizens generally have so openly expressed the desire that the paving of Bull street with asphalt should be continued to the park, it is to be hoped that Council will be able to arrange for the accomplishment of the work at an early date."

With sufficient rights-of-way available, Bull Street has transitioned seamlessly from the horse-and-buggy era to the automotive age. Today, a variety of transportation options, both motorized and nonmotorized, exist along the street. Chatam Area Transit offers a free shuttle that runs along parts of Bull Street and throughout the historic district. The downtown loop bus crosses Bull Street, running east on Broughton and west on Oglethorpe. Private trolley buses offer tours of the downtown. Taxis, pedi-cabs, and bicycles also travel the street.

To encourage walking, the city has opened a parking lot four blocks from Bull Street. City workers are encouraged to park there and take the free shuttle to the core. Many, however, choose to walk. Granite curbs, brick sidewalks,

Zoned for mixed use, Bull Street is home to religious congregations, government agencies, entrepreneurs, corporations, and local residents.

and public and private landscape efforts enhance the streetscape and attract tourists. The architecture, tree canopies, coffee shops, restaurants, and public squares make it one of the best downtown streets for strolling, power walking, and jogging.

Zoned for mixed use, Bull Street is home to religious congregations, government agencies, entrepreneurs, corporations, and local residents. There are no vacant properties here. The Bull Street corridor features outstanding examples of Greek Revival, Italianate, Second Empire, and Postmodern architecture, giving the feeling that the street has evolved over time.

Public, sacred, commercial, and private buildings line Bull Street. Savannah's main library, featuring a neoclassic design by H.W. Witcover, opened to much fanfare in 1916. The street also is home to: City Hall; the birthplace of Juliette Gordon Low, founder of the Girl Scouts; and the historic Savannah Theatre, an 1818 structure by William Jay, who would later design the Telfair mansion on Barnard Street.

Historic Christ Church, Bull Street Baptist Church, and Temple Mickve Israel are among the houses of worship found on Bull Street. The nation's third oldest and only purely Gothic Revival synagogue, Temple Mickve Israel, was consecrated in 1878. Its location on Monterey Square is directly across from Mercer House, an Italianate mansion that served as the centerpiece for the novel *Midnight in the Garden of Good and Evil.*

As Savannah looks to its future, the city has put in place height and design standards to help ensure that new infill development along Bull Street is compatible with existing buildings. Underground parking is encouraged as are environmentally sound practices, such as green roofs.

Having sustained economic, physical, political, and societal pressures for nearly three centuries, Bull Street continues to adapt to contemporary uses, the result of an innovative plan that still serves as a model for new urban developments.

Courtesy of Chatham County-Savannah Metropolitan Planning Commission

*(Above) This Middle-Eastern-looking storefront is indicative of the variety of architectural styles to be found along this street, which includes great examples of Greek Revival, Italianate, Second Empire, and even Postmodern architecture.
(Below) You can picture yourself relaxing at this corner coffee shop on Bull Street, taking in the beautiful weather, architecture, and urban forest, and listening to the clop of a horse's hooves in the street.*

Charlotte Moore

Keeping with the spirit of an artist's colony, the houses along Canyon Road are marked by vibrant colors, making them an additional site for those who come to view and buy the art displayed and sold here.

Joe Burns

CHAPTER 3

Canyon Road
Santa Fe, New Mexico

Once a route used by Native Americans to access spiritual sites in the Sangre de Cristo Mountains, Canyon Road today is home to one of the nation's most vibrant art markets. Attracting more than 1.5 million visitors each year, this street is famous for a historic style, character, and charm celebrated by visitors and locals alike.

The 1.5-mile stretch of Canyon Road between Paseo de Peralta and Cristo Rey Church is a narrow corridor filled with one-story, common-walled structures that offers glimpses into the city's roots—the ancient village streets of Mexico, Spain, and Moorish Africa. Authentic adobe architecture is creatively interspersed with buildings in the Spanish-Pueblo Revival or American territorial styles, and many of the modest two- or three-room dwellings date back more than 100 years.

*In keeping with the 1912 "City Different" plan, an effort was made
by local leaders to identify Santa Fe style.*

Courtesy Paloheimo Collection

*Canyon Road was actually unpaved until
1960. This historic photo gives one a real
feel for what the road must have been like
before modernization.*

Joe Burns

*A resident's adobe wall under repair.
Such houses sit shoulder to shoulder
with restaurants and bars where one can
find world-class Spanish classical guitar,
flamenco, and jazz. The combination keeps
the road lively and unique.*

The successful preservation of this historic road has its roots in Santa Fe's 1912 "City Different" plan. Adopted shortly after New Mexico was granted statehood, the plan, which lacked any real teeth, was intended to "guard the old streets against any change that will affect their appearance."

In keeping with the plan's theme, "the City Different," an effort was made by local leaders to identify Santa Fe style, with its generally flat roofs, and distinguish it from other popular architectural styles of the times, such as the sloping-roofed California Mission. Several photographers recorded unifying features to help document what would eventually become known as Spanish-Pueblo Revival architecture.

This narrow and windy road, unpaved until 1960, provides a unique sense of place. "Canyon Road has an intimate feel," says Jerry Porter, retired Santa Fe city planner. "Numerous buildings are set right at the street edge."

That intimacy, combined with one-story buildings and narrow sidewalks, creates an inviting experience for pedestrians. Old trees line and shade the streets; native landscaping, such as wildflowers and sage brushes, enrich the vistas; and uneven juniper pole "coyote fences" (named after the animals that they are meant to keep out) aptly demonstrate the region's unique Southwestern style. Perhaps most stunning are the strong contrasts and colors: turquoise skies mix with brown adobe walls, snow-capped mountain peaks rise above rooftops. The buildings themselves are works of art—doors and gates all painted in rich shades of turquoise, purple, red, and yellow.

Throughout much of its history, Canyon Road existed as a quiet farming community on the city's outskirts. Its turning point came in the 1920s when a group of painters settled on the then dirt road and began selling artwork from their homes. The presence of these nationally recognized artists, known as "Los Cinco Pintores," slowly transformed Canyon Road into a thriving art community.

To accommodate this transformation and preserve its architectural heritage, the city made two important planning decisions. First, it adopted the Historic Style Ordinance in 1957, codifying the elements of the 1912 plan. The ordinance was championed by Irene von Horvath, an architect, artist, and member of the city's planning commission from 1955 to 1967, and drafted by Pulitzer Prize winning author Oliver LaFarge and architect John Gaw Meem. The ordinance was strengthened in 1992 when it was expanded to protect existing buildings and streetscapes rather than just overseeing new construction and renovations.

Canyon Road is a vital component of Santa Fe's art-based economy that provides some 2,500 jobs and $54 million in annual tax revenues.

(Left) Dozens of old adobe and Spanish colonial houses have been converted to galleries and studios offering sculpture both for sale and as part of the street's unique look. (Below) An overlay zone, known as Arts and Crafts Residential Compound-8, affects the western two-thirds of lower Canyon Road, protecting galleries, like the Waxlander Gallery and Sculpture Garden.

A second major planning decision, in 1962, established Canyon Road as a Residential Arts and Crafts District. This zoning technique allowed local artists to sell their works from their homes. In 1947, there were two art galleries in Santa Fe. By 1964, the road was home to nine of the city's 12 galleries.

Today, dozens of old adobes and traditional Spanish colonials have been converted into galleries and studios, many featuring traditional and contemporary Native American and Spanish arts, crafts, and sculpture. Shoulder to shoulder with restaurants and bars where one can find world-class Spanish classical guitar, flamenco, and jazz, the combination keeps the road lively and unique. While Canyon Road, like many parts of Santa Fe, has faced challenges of affordability, it also is a vital component of the city's art-based economy that provides some 2,500 jobs and $54 million in annual tax revenues.

To protect portions of Canyon Road from high-density development, the city changed the zoning along the street in the 1980s. The resulting overlay zone, known as Arts and Crafts Residential Compound-8, affects the western two-thirds of lower Canyon Road, according to Reed Liming, the city's long-range planning director. "This downzoning reduced the allowable density from 21 to eight units per acre," he said. "The intent is to prevent wholesale redevelopment."

Canyon Road preservation efforts received a boost in 1995 when the New Mexico General Assembly approved the Cultural Properties Preservation Easement Act. Under terms of an easement, the property owner gives up certain development rights (e.g., the right to demolish or subdivide the property) but retains ownership and possession of the property. The nonprofit, easement recipient

Photos by Joe Burns

assumes responsibility for preserving the structure as well as monitoring and enforcing the easement in perpetuity. Tax benefits for landowners willing to preserve cultural properties were enhanced in 2003.

The Historic Santa Fe Foundation has established a program for accepting easements and a Stewardship Fund to cover the expenses of monitoring and enforcing easements. One of several easements received to date, 728 Canyon Road, had been home to von Horvath, the former planning commissioner, since 1954.

Style, character, and charm, long the hallmarks of Canyon Road, help set this street apart. While its evolution is not complete, Canyon Road's future looks bright. Creative planning, zoning, and preservation programs are enabling this historic street to embrace the future without losing sight of its past.

The Tivoli Theater, built in 1924, was one of many buildings along the Delmar Loop that was revitalized by an active local businessman, Joe Edwards. He purchased and restored the theater in 1993.

Alise O'Brien

CHAPTER 4

Delmar Loop
University City and St. Louis, Missouri

Not terribly long ago, the Delmar Loop was nothing more than a strip of mostly vacant, boarded-up storefronts. Missing was the energy and vitality of today's street, an eclectic arts, entertainment, and shopping district with more than 140 boutiques, eateries, dining, and other shops spanning the border of two Missouri municipalities.

The economic backbone of the area, the Delmar Loop derives its name from the turnaround that once enabled streetcars to return from University City to nearby St. Louis. This six-block stretch of Delmar Boulevard runs from westernmost St. Louis to the Lion Gates, two massive, concrete, feline structures that mark the entrance to University City's residential area.

Both tourists and local residents frequent the boulevard's numerous galleries, restaurants, and nightclubs. Locals come to The Loop on foot while others arrive by MetroLink, the area's successful rail system. If Loop advocates are successful, a trolley eventually will shuttle passengers between the Missouri History Museum in Forest Park and Delmar Boulevard. A $1.5 million feasibility study is expected to be completed in early 2009.

Delmar Boulevard was established in 1891 after the state legislature empowered St. Louis to create a network of boulevards by ordinance. . .spurring their development as major thoroughfares.

Courtesy of The Historical Society of University City, Missouri

The Delmar Loop derives its name from the turnaround that once enabled streetcars to return from University City to nearby St. Louis. This is what that turnaround looked like circa 1900.

Joe Edwards

Delmar Loop's comeback began in earnest in 1972 when Joe Edwards and his wife opened Blueberry Hill, a pub. In 1980, he helped create a special taxing district to raise money for streetscape enhancements that further improved the Loop.

By the mid-1880s, horse-drawn trolley service was a fixture on what was first known as Bonhomme Road, transporting St. Louisians to area attractions such as the Delmar Rack Track and the Delmar Garden Amusement Park. Delmar Boulevard was established in 1891 after the state legislature empowered St. Louis to create a network of boulevards by ordinance. This legal definition provided a new level of importance to these streets, spurring their development as major thoroughfares and encouraging St. Louis's westward expansion. After University City incorporated in 1906, shops, offices, and apartments replaced the entertainment venues. By the 1930s, The Loop was a thriving retail area. Its well-planned streets and variety of land uses made it especially attractive to pedestrians.

The arrival of suburban shopping malls in the 1950s took its toll on the street. As the area began to decline, a revitalization plan channeled nearly $8 million into the area, allowing University City to demolish substandard buildings and offer low-interest loans for renovation projects. The city widened sidewalks and narrowed streets to slow traffic and create space for outdoor cafes.

Probably the city's most prescient decision in the 1960s was to reserve all streetfront building space for retail, restaurants, shops, and galleries. Existing office tenants were grandfathered in, but when a first-floor office was vacated, landlords could rent only to commercial users. This led to more than 140 boutiques, eateries, and entertainment venues along the boulevard between Des Peres and Trinity.

Despite the zoning change and streetscape improvements, the area remained deserted. The comeback began in earnest in 1972 when a young entrepreneur and his wife opened Blueberry Hill, a neighborhood pub. Owner Joe Edwards organized local business owners. In 1980, he helped create a special taxing district to raise money for streetscape enhancements that included dusk-to-dawn lighting in alleys, flower planters, and unique, eye-catching holiday decorations and store awnings. In 2006, voters approved an additional one-quarter of 1 percent retail sales tax, portions of which are earmarked for street improvements and the proposed trolley.

After fire destroyed the area's last remaining grocery store in the early 1970s, residents rallied. Shortly thereafter, construction began on the Market in the Loop, an outdoor farmer's market. Some 15 years later, an indoor section of the market, fronting on Delmar opened. About that time, the city sold the market to a businessman who refurbished the building and brought in new vendors. Today, the market offers fresh fruits and vegetables along with ready-to-eat foods. The indoor section houses a fish

The "Delmar Design District" was created to provide one-stop shopping by consolidating the activities of Saint Louis's design-related wholesalers, retailers, and service providers within one region of the city.

market; hamburger stand; pizzeria; American BBQ; Chinese and Nigerian food kiosks; and bead and jewelry shops.

The Loop's placement on the National Register of Historic Places in 1984 led to an increase in renovations as developers qualified for federal tax breaks. As new businesses opened along the Delmar Loop, Edwards and others became more involved in redevelopment efforts. This, in turn, attracted more residents to houses that range in price from $50,000 to $1 million.

The residential area of The Loop includes many apartment buildings constructed in 1900, just prior to the opening of the St. Louis World's Fair. Many of these buildings also house commercial activities.

Following the 1993 opening of the MetroLink station, Edwards purchased and restored the 1924 Tivoli Theatre. In 2000, he opened The Pageant, a concert nightclub on the Delmar Loop, extending the thriving retail and entertainment district into neighboring St. Louis. Across the street from The Pageant now sits the Regional Arts Commission's $11 million Cultural Resource Center. A boutique hotel is being planned for a late 2008 grand opening.

Embedded in the sidewalk along Delmar Boulevard are large brass stars, each accompanied by a bronze plaque commemorating the life and achievements of extraordinary individuals who are associated with St. Louis. Since the Walk of Fame opened in 1989, more than 100 men and women of distinction, including Ulysses S. Grant, Scott Joplin, Stan Musial, and Charles A. Lindbergh, have been honored with a star.

Recent efforts have focused on marketing a stretch of Delmar Boulevard, just east of The Loop between the MetroLink station and De Baliviere Avenue, as the "Delmar Design District." Like those in Chicago, Washington, D.C., and New York, this district was created to provide one-stop shopping by consolidating the activities of Saint Louis's design-related wholesalers, retailers, and service providers within one region of the city.

The Loop also hosts several annual festivals and events such as Love in the Loop on Valentine's Day, the Gateway Cup Bicycle Race during Labor Day weekend, the Loop in Motion arts festival in October, and the Loop Holiday Walk the first Saturday in December. These events bring thousands of visitors and residents to the area throughout the year.

The sustained efforts of local business and government combined with community support have fueled the revitalization of the Delmar Loop. This is not a cloned street, but a vibrant place with a character of its own. As The Loop community grows physically and economically, it seeks to attract businesses that complement and build on the street's unique identity, continuing its prosperity and vitality.

No city known for its historical role in music-making would be complete without street musicians. This Delmar Loop sax man is just one of many.

Andrea Riganti

MBK (old skool)

The Walk of Fame opened on Delmar Loop in 1989. More than 100 men and women of distinction have been honored, including Chuck Berry, who has come back from time to time to perform for hometown crowds.

The imposing County Courthouse anchors one of Main Street's corners.

Gene Bunnell

CHAPTER 5

Main Street
Northampton, Massachusetts

Whether coming from the east or west, there's never a doubt that one has reached Northampton's Main Street. "There's a sense of place, walkability, and an eclectic mix of architectural styles. This isn't a homogeneous place," said the city's former planning director Gene Bunnell, now an associate professor at the State University of New York, Albany.

Main Street adheres essentially to the same path that was laid out following the city's founding as a Puritan settlement in 1654. Rather than relying on the traditional grid typical of many downtowns, Northampton's streets follow the topography of the land. As Main Street meanders through downtown, its curves close off the vista, providing definition to distinct spaces.

To get people out of their cars and onto Main Street, planners were instrumental in the development of a unique parking structure that blends seamlessly with the historic urban fabric.

Main Street follows nearly the same path as it did when the city was founded as a Puritan settlement in 1654. Rather than relying on the traditional grid typical of many downtowns, Northampton's streets follow the topography of the land.

Both ends of Main Street acknowledge one's arrival, but the eastern entry practically defines the term "gateway," according to Bunnell, who was Northampton's planning director in the 1980s. "Once you cross the Connecticut River, you'll pass through an area that's mostly residential. You'll go 'round a bend before passing under a railroad trestle," he said. "It's like going through the archway of a walled city."

Over the years, public art has been used to enhance the trestle's aesthetics. The 1980s featured two murals. One showed an urban fabric to those entering the city. On the other side, for those leaving, was a rural landscape and river. Today there's a sculpture featuring a railroad theme.

The mix of architectural styles combined with current uses—boutiques, galleries, coffee houses, and restaurants—creates visual interest and encourages people to walk, gather, and interact.

Coming from the west, travelers are treated to a scenic view of the downtown. Beyond Smith College, there's a bend in the road and a drop in elevation. The view encompasses the beautiful Holyoke range as well as the city.

While 19th century buildings command the streetscape, it's the mix of architectural styles combined with current uses—boutiques, galleries, coffee houses, and restaurants—that create visual interest and encourage people to walk, gather, and interact. Public and civic structures occupy the most visually prominent locations and dominate the skyline due to zoning that prohibits taller structures. Until 1980, eight-story buildings were allowed in the downtown. Since then, the allowable height has been reduced to five stories. New buildings are required to maintain alignment with existing structures.

To get people out of their cars and onto Main Street, planners were instrumental in the development of a unique parking structure that blends seamlessly with the historic urban fabric. The garage made it possible for the city to allow Main Street building owners to expand or modify without having to provide additional parking. This has served as an incentive to owners of one-level structures to build a second story, thereby enhancing the visual appeal of the streetscape. Situated behind Thornes Marketplace, the five-level garage features a walkway that connects to the midlevel of a five-story commercial building at 150 Main Street and its 25 shops, restaurants, galleries, studios, and businesses.

Thornes has been a cornerstone of downtown Northampton for more than a century. Pressed tin ceilings, hardwood floors, stained glass windows, walnut center staircase, and a host of other classic Victorian details give the space an old world charm. The marketplace, which was a department store from 1873 to 1973, also helped kick off a renaissance in the downtown.

Northampton has provided public investment for affordable housing, fostering the redevelopment of empty public buildings back into productive use.

The advent of strip shopping malls in the 1950s and, later, indoor malls, threatened the vitality of Main Street. As many traditional anchors—department and hardware stores for example—closed up shop, downtown Northampton struggled.

In the mid- to late-1970s, the interior of the old McCallum's Department Store was subdivided and leased to individual shop owners. The idea was to create a place with the energy, sights, smells, and sounds of an old-world marketplace. Over the past three decades, Thornes has served as an incubator of sorts as several shop owners have moved into larger spaces on Main Street, their shops at the marketplace snapped up by new entrepreneurs.

Today, retail vacancy rates along Main Street are extremely low and the upper floors of buildings are filled with offices and residences. More than 20 percent of downtown residents live within a half mile of the center of downtown and 41 percent live within a mile. While the area includes a wide variety of incomes and housing stock, nearly 70 percent of all housing units within one mile of the heart of the central business district are rental.

Design integrity and pedestrian orientation are considered Main Street's strongest unifying features. A 1980s streetscape program sent utility lines underground, eliminating poles. That change, combined with a solid wall of building fronts, provides an uninterrupted, continuous facade along Main Street. Planners have discouraged uses that generate heavy vehicular traffic. Some of those uses (automobile sales and services) are prohibited, while others (take-out restaurants) require a special use permit. The result is a sense of liveliness day and night, weekday and weekend.

In recent years, a reduction in minimum required lot dimensions has encouraged development, which would otherwise not be allowed, to fill gaps on small, narrow lots. The city also has provided public investment for affordable housing, fostering the redevelopment of empty public buildings back into productive use, and has focused on brownfield revitalization of contaminated downtown sites. All of these changes have generated new activity on and around Main Street.

The success of Northampton's Main Street has led to the revitalization of other, contiguous areas within the city. Over the past decade, as the availability of moderately priced retail space has declined, a new wave of redevelopment has come to nearby Pleasant Street and other commercial areas off Main Street.

Singled out as one of the top 25 arts destinations by *American Style Magazine*, Main Street's success comes as much from what city policies and planning efforts have prevented from happening as what they've allowed to happen. Main Street is a tribute to decades of successful economic and land-use planning efforts in Northampton.

Kirsten Martin

Northampton began a streetscape program in the 1980s that put utility lines underground, eliminating overhead wires and utility poles.

Kirsten Martin

Main Street's success has meant extremely low vacancy rates for ground-floor businesses as well as the offices and residences above them.

Designated a National Historic Landmark in 1997, Monument Avenue emphasizes order, symmetry, hierarchy, and planning, and, as its name implies, monuments. This is the Jefferson Davis monument.

CHAPTER 6

Monument Avenue
Richmond, Virginia

Few streets in the United States can match the splendor of Monument Avenue in Richmond, Virginia. Designated a National Historic Landmark in 1997, the avenue, a linear corridor, is an excellent example of the late nineteenth century, Beaux-Arts inspired, urban boulevard design that emphasizes order, symmetry, hierarchy, and planning.

This 1.5-mile extension of downtown's Franklin Street has, as its eastern border, the state capitol building, which was designed by Thomas Jefferson and built in 1785. Entering Richmond from the west, the avenue provides a stunningly unified procession to the denouement of Capitol Square.

The avenue's 130-foot-wide right-of-way contains a 40-foot, median lined with stately oaks and maples. As a result of the uniform tree spacing—between 36 and 40 feet—block after block features a lush, green canopy that shields walkers and joggers from the summer sun. The grand avenue includes 36-foot-wide, two-lane streets and double-wide, 10-foot sidewalks.

Interspersed at key cross streets are six memorials that pay tribute to the past (Civil War General Robert E. Lee and four Confederate contemporaries) and the present (Arthur Ashe, an African-American son of Richmond, humanitarian, and tennis champion). All of the monuments along the street are situated on islands in the middle of the intersections.

*Monument Avenue is replete with examples from the late nineteenth and early twentieth centuries,
including Colonial Revival, Craftsman, Classical Revival, Mediterranean, Romanesque, and Tudor Revival.*

MONUMENT AVENUE AND LEE MONUMENT, RICHMOND, VA.

An aerial view of Monument Avenue on an old postcard.

Courtesy of Shutterstock

The monument to J.E.B. Stuart, a Confederate general, is 30 feet from where he was mortally wounded in 1864. The First English Lutheran Church, a fine example of Neo-Gothic style, is in the background.

It is the diversity of architecture that gives Monument Avenue much of its character. The boulevard is replete with examples from the late nineteenth and early twentieth centuries, including Colonial Revival, Craftsman, Classical Revival, Mediterranean, Romanesque, and Tudor Revival. The use of similar construction materials, cornice lines, setbacks, and other repetitive visual devices brings a high level of compatibility to the assortment of buildings along the avenue, which was a showcase for builders and architects. The percentage of houses on Monument Avenue designed by architects is significantly higher than in the surrounding Fan and Grace districts.

While mansions are common, smaller residences, townhouses, condos, and apartment buildings also line the avenue. As a result, a mix of people with varied economic and social backgrounds resides here.

Several institutions also chose to locate on Monument Avenue. Stuart Circle Hospital was built in 1913. Six Protestant congregations erected churches, and a private girls school constructed a building as well.

Monument Avenue is one of the most intensely used pedestrian spaces in Richmond, attracting joggers, walkers, festival-goers, and thousands of tourists annually. The avenue's hardscape and landscape features combine to enhance the pedestrian experience while ornamental lighting allows for around-the-clock use and improves safety. Porches and small front yards encourage human interaction.

While public transportation exists in Richmond, Monument Avenue, with its numerous traffic circles, was never intended to accommodate transit routes. Public transit runs parallel to the avenue, a few blocks north and south, ensuring that the surrounding neighborhoods are served.

The original plan for Monument Avenue stemmed from the desire of many Richmonders to find a suitably impressive location for a monument to Lee. In 1886, a wealthy landowner, Otway Allen, commissioned a plan for a grand avenue—one that would not only pay tribute to Confederate heroes but showcase the city's sophistication and prosperity. The plan also encouraged residential development west of Richmond where Allen had amassed land.

Since its inception, Monument Avenue has been subject to controversy. The selection of property belonging to Allen's family as the site for the initial monument to Lee engendered much debate about its isolated location, the expenditure of city funds to design and pave new streets, and the commercialism inherent in using a memorial to promote residential development. Even after the cornerstone was laid on October 27, 1887, the plan for Monument Avenue continued to be adjusted.

Due to a recession in the 1890s, the first house was not built on the avenue until 1901, 11 years after the dedica-

With the support of a growing preservation movement in the U.S., Monument Avenue became a part of the public agenda when it was designated a City of Richmond Old and Historic District.

(Left) Monument Avenue's landscape features enhance the pedestrian experience. Ornamental lighting on the avenue allows for around-the-clock use and improves safety. (Below) While many have viewed Monument Avenue as a shrine to the Confederacy, the Arthur Ashe memorial reasserted the boulevard's commitment to heroism.

tion of the Lee memorial. The bulk of the houses were constructed by 1930, and no buildings of architectural significance were erected after 1947.

Monument Avenue declined after World War II as the suburbs replaced urban neighborhoods as the American ideal. During the 1950s, many of the larger houses were transformed into apartments, nursing homes, and doctors' offices as maintenance and upkeep became issues for many families. Crime increased.

The construction of a modern doctor's office—dark and out of scale with surrounding structures—served as a rallying point for the avenue's supporters in 1955. Various plans were debated. Some would have created a more efficient commuter thoroughfare by widening the street, cutting down trees, and moving monuments. Others would have honored the avenue's history, staying true to its founders' intent.

In 1968, with paving machines set to cover the road's original Belgian asphalt paving blocks, homeowner Helen Marie Taylor stepped in front of the vehicles to prevent what many saw as an irreparable assault on the avenue's historic character. Those who viewed Monument Avenue primarily as a commuter route into the city often complained about the noise that was created when driving over the aesthetically pleasing blocks.

Soon after, with the support of a growing preservation movement in the U.S., the history of the avenue became a part of the public agenda when it was designated a City of Richmond Old and Historic District.

Since Taylor made her stand, deteriorating mansions along the avenue have been restored; buildings converted to commercial use have been returned to residences; and, more recently, an old apartment building once used for office space is now an assisted living facility, providing opportunities for aging in place.

The avenue's historical intent and its role in twenty-first century Richmond was again subject to debate when, in 1995, the street was proposed as the site for a monument to the tennis legend Ashe. The discussions echoed those of previous eras. The appropriateness of the site was questioned, as was whether a monument to a tennis player fit the avenue's existing theme. While many have viewed Monument Avenue as a shrine to the Confederacy, the Ashe memorial reasserted the boulevard's commitment to heroism.

Today, the boulevard remains enormously popular with pedestrians, says Richmond planner T. Tyler Potterfield, whether it's jogging, dog walking, marching in or viewing the annual Easter parade, or running in a 10K race. "It's just a very grand space," he says, "but people feel very comfortable with it. It's not daunting."

No museum piece, yet rich in history, Monument Avenue instills a sense of the past with the present, making even an ordinary ride or everyday stroll down this boulevard something extraordinary and long remembered.

One of the country's most beloved avenues, North Michigan's continuing evolution is testimony to the planning, design, and community involvement needed to sustain a world-class street.

Sarah Amaryllis Fleming

CHAPTER 7

North Michigan Avenue
Chicago, Illinois

Chicago's North Michigan Avenue is a study in contrasts—a major commercial corridor where history and modernity strike a delicate balance. One of the country's most beloved avenues, North Michigan's continuing evolution is testimony to the planning, design, and community involvement needed to sustain a world-class street.

Envisioned as the Midwest equivalent of the Champs Elysees in Paris, North Michigan Avenue first appeared in Daniel Burnham and Edward Bennett's 1909 Plan of Chicago. The plan, an embodiment of the City Beautiful movement, was embraced by civic, business, and political leaders. At that time, the avenue was known as Pine Street, a quiet road with just a few houses and walk-up apartments. In 1913, the city's voters approved a bond issue to finance improvements needed to extend Michigan Avenue to the north side of the Chicago River.

As North Michigan Avenue grew to include high-rise office buildings, luxury retail merchants, hoteliers, and corporate headquarters, a local real estate developer dubbed it the Magnificent Mile.

This photo was taken just five years after the city opted to eliminate the 10-story height limit on the avenue. The city's new limit was 264 feet.

That same year, a group of Chicago businessmen banded together to plan and build what would become the city's most fashionable street. The association not only agreed on the kinds of businesses it wanted to attract—no warehouses or saloons—but the types of architectural detailing it wanted to encourage. The only element not to withstand the 20-year agreement was the 10-story building height limit, eliminated in 1923 when the city's zoning code allowed heights of 264 feet on North Michigan. Land acquisition was completed by 1918 and, two years later, the Michigan Avenue Bridge opened. The beautiful bascule bridge, designated a city landmark in 1991, is modeled on the Pont Alexandre III in Paris. Rapid development followed. Soon after the bridge's dedication, the Drake Hotel opened on the northern end as did the Wrigley building to the south. Other notable and architecturally significant buildings that followed included the Allerton Hotel, the Tribune Tower, and the Medinah Athletic Club.

As the avenue grew to include high-rise office buildings, luxury retail merchants, hoteliers, and corporate headquarters, a local real estate developer dubbed it the Magnificent Mile. The name stuck and, in 2001, it was trademarked.

During the Great Depression, construction along North Michigan Avenue ceased. For more than three decades the street seemed frozen in time. A building boom in the 1970s resulted in the loss of several historic structures and served as a rallying cry for local preservationists. A plan to designate North Michigan Avenue as a National Register Historic District failed when the Illinois Historic Preservation Agency determined that the street had lost too many historic buildings to qualify.

Since the late 1980s, the focus has been on preserving individual buildings along the Magnificent Mile. All but two of the avenue's current nine landmarks, which include the Palmolive and McGraw-Hill buildings, Tribune Tower, and the Women's Athletic Club, were so designated by the city after historic district status was denied.

More recently, debate has centered on the definition of preservation. Developers have proposed dismantling a 1920s-era building on the Magnificent Mile and saving the stone front. After demolishing the 11-story structure, they would erect a new 40-story, luxury condo building and reapply the façade. Preservation groups claim the practice makes a mockery of the regulatory process and creates an illusion of history. As the city, businesses, and residents grapple with the issue, their passion for North Michigan Avenue and its future is evident.

The Magnificent Mile is home to small open spaces and parks like this one surrounding the old Chicago Water Tower, a castle-like structure that survived the Great Fire of 1871.

Although a dense, urban corridor with numerous skyscrapers, North Michigan has managed to avoid the canyon effect. Thoughtful design by some of the world's foremost architectural firms allows light and air to permeate the avenue. For example, several high-rise buildings have one or more setbacks on the way up that allow towers to ascend gracefully from massive bases.

Despite its grand scale, North Michigan Avenue has a beauty and charm that attract pedestrians en masse. Ma-

A seven-block urban wonderland, North Michigan Avenue demonstrates what planning, greening, and positive public-private partnerships can create.

ture, stately elm trees complement the skyscrapers. Locust and pear trees along with seasonal plantings create a garden-like environment as calming as it is visually stunning. These privately financed beautification efforts were introduced in the 1940s by a local developer. Today it is not unusual for property owners to engage in friendly landscaping competitions. The avenue is home to small open spaces and parks, such as that surrounding the old Chicago Water Tower, a castle-like structure that survived the Great Fire of 1871.

Each holiday season, the magnificent mile is aglow, the result of a million lights on 200 of the street's finest trees. Other seasonal events draw attention to the avenue's landscaping. Spring is marked by tulip days, when hundreds of thousands of tulips bloom in 52 gardens up and down the street.

North Michigan Avenue is a heavily traveled street. It has six lanes for vehicles, broad, bustling sidewalks

jewelry shop adjoins a high-tech electronics store. A few blocks away, a furrier sits across the street from a record store flanked by shops selling upscale apparel. Still, rents along the avenue are among the priciest in the nation. Only four U.S. cities have street-level retail more expensive than the Magnificent Mile's average of $250 per square foot, according to *Retail Real Estate Highlights*, a 2007 report by Colliers International.

Planning has been important to Michigan Avenue's development since its inception. While there is no formal, city-endorsed plan for the corridor, many plans have been privately sponsored and funded by local building and business owners. The first, *A Program for North Michigan Avenue*, was prepared in 1967. Thirty years later, a fourth plan, *Vision 2012: Applauding Our Past, Enhancing Our Present, Preparing for the Future*, was released.

(Above) Christmas lights up North Michigan Avenue every year. (Left) Besides Christmas, other seasonal events serve to enliven the avenue's landscaping, including tulip days, when 52 gardens of tulips bloom up and down the street.

for pedestrians, and access to the subway for residents, tourists, and commuters. Numerous buses and seasonal trolleys serve the avenue along with Chicago River tour boats and a water taxi service in season.

The range of transportation options brings thousands to the street every day, and North Michigan Avenue does not disappoint. While known for its high-end retail, five-star hotels, fine dining, and nightlife, the Magnificent Mile offers something for everyone. Here, an elegant

The City of Chicago revised its zoning code in the 1980s to allow for the infill of open-air building arcades, created with 1970s zoning bonuses, with high-end retail space. A special sign district, established in 1997, ensures high-quality signage along the Magnificent Mile.

A seven-block urban wonderland, North Michigan Avenue demonstrates what planning, greening, and positive public-private partnerships can create—one of America's leading great streets.

The Colony Hotel is one of many Art Deco hotels whose architecture communicates that you are on beautiful Ocean Drive in Miami Beach, a street unlike any other.

COLONY
HOTEL

736

J. McNally

CHAPTER 8

Ocean Drive
Miami, Florida

Home to the largest concentration of Art Deco buildings in the United States, Ocean Drive in Miami Beach might well be a strip of modern-day, high-rise hotels and condos were it not for a grassroots historic preservation and planning effort. Over several decades, this citizen-led endeavor turned around the fortunes of a once-glamorous 10-block drive that had hit hard times.

Ocean Drive lies a block east of the city's main thoroughfare. Running north-south between 5th and 15th Streets, this section of road consists of a few dozen hotels and apartment buildings, built primarily in the 1930s, that are prime examples of pre-war modernism. These vividly colored buildings, none taller than 10 stories, represent an era when Miami Beach was promoted as a tropical playground. Most of the Art Deco structures are easily discernible, with rounded masonry designs, flat roofs and lively color palettes—everything from pastel to neon.

Architects designed hundreds of buildings in the Art Deco style that went up during the 1930s, giving South Beach a remarkably uniform appearance.

Courtesy of The City of Miami Beach Archives

During the two decades after its incorporation in 1915, Miami Beach became home to more than 1,000 Mediterranean Revival, Art Deco, and Streamline Moderne hotels, apartments, and other buildings. Here is the view of Ocean Drive in 1924.

It was only a few short years after Miami Beach was incorporated in 1915 that the wealthy and well-heeled, including Harvey Firestone and J.C. Penney, took up residence here. During the next two decades, more than 1,000 Mediterranean Revival, Art Deco, and Streamline Moderne hotels, apartments, and other buildings would be constructed, a legacy no other city could match.

During the 1930s, while much of the nation suffered through the Great Depression, Miami Beach's tourist-driven economy boomed. A small number of architects designed hundreds of buildings in the Art Deco style that went up during the 1930s, giving South Beach a remarkably uniform appearance. Depression-era buildings, designed in a more sober Streamline style, have little ornamentation and a very flat, machine-like look. Hallmarks of this particular phase of Art Deco include rounded corners, banded stripes, porthole windows, and lots of glass block.

Prosperity continued into the 1960s, when Jackie Gleason began taping his weekly variety show in Miami Beach. By the end of the decade, with a recession underway, hotels along Ocean Drive entered a more than 20-year period of decline, abandonment, and demolition. Some at the time believed the only solution was to level all of the period buildings and construct a modern-day Venice with canals, restaurants, high-rise hotels, condominiums, and retail shops.

Recognizing the incalculable worth of the city's stock of Art Deco buildings, including those along Ocean Drive, was citizen advocate Barbara Capitman. A writer and former newspaper reporter who moved to Miami Beach from New York City, she founded the Miami Design Preservation League in 1976 to protect and restore the city's Art Deco heritage. Capitman's efforts led to the area's 1979 federal designation as the Miami Beach Architectural Historic District, popularly known as the "Art Deco District." It was the nation's first, twentieth century historic district.

The federal designation was just the first step. Gaining public, business, and political support for the enactment of meaningful historic area protection ordinances would take another decade.

In 1984, the Miami Beach Planning Department released a study, based on nine months of community meetings and internal analysis, that recommended establishment of a mixed-use entertainment district and the complete rehabilitation of a structure before it could become eligible for the new uses permitted in the district. The establishment of design review guidelines, limits on new construction, and incentives to promote reinvestment also were suggested. *Ocean Drive: A Planning and Urban Design Strategy* was well received by the

Ocean Drive: A Planning and Urban Design Strategy, *the plan for the street, came out of a process in the early 1980s that established design review guidelines, limits on new construction, and incentives to promote reinvestment. The plan won an honorable mention from APA.*

Courtesy of CTPEKO3A

Art Deco may be South Beach's heart, but Ocean Drive is its soul. From dawn to dusk, sun worshippers, tourists, retirees, body builders, and the occasional celebrity fill the sidewalks.

community. After its adoption in 1985, the plan received numerous awards including an honorable mention from the American Planning Association.

As plan recommendations gradually were implemented and incentives and regulations put in place, local businesses formed the Ocean Drive Association with the primary purpose of garnering public support for a $3 million bond to fund improvements to the streetscape. The debt would be shared equally by the city and property owners, who would have 20 years to repay the funds. "This one act was pivotal in the revitalization of South Beach," says Tony Goldman a developer and strong advocate of historic preserva-

Built primarily in the 1930s, the hotels along Ocean Drive are prime examples of pre-war modernism. Vividly colored, none taller than 10 stories, the structures feature rounded masonry designs and flat roofs.

Lummus Park separates Ocean Drive from the beach. This former plantation acreage is a popular spot for volleyball, inline skating, strolling, and people-watching.

tion who headed the association in 1986, "because it allowed us to realize our vision of a promenade—a Riviera—America's Riviera."

With funds available for implementation, the city and property owners spent three years transforming the street. A 20-foot-wide promenade and an outdoor concert stage were constructed along the oceanfront (east) side of the street. Sidewalks on the west side were expanded to allow for al fresco dining. As outdoor cafes grew in number, the city derived additional income through a tax on tables.

Separating Ocean Drive from the white sand beach is Lummus Park. Sold to the city in 1920, this former plantation acreage is a popular spot for volleyball, inline skating, strolling, and people-watching. Palm trees provide a respite from the sun, and the calm of the lush foliage provides a welcome counterpoint to the nearly continuous activity along Ocean Drive. The park hosts festivals as well as concerts by many big-name performers. Improvements, including new plantings, bike racks, trash receptacles, and restrooms compatible in design with the surrounding district, were completed in 2006.

Art Deco may be South Beach's heart, but Ocean Drive is its soul. From dawn to dusk, sun worshippers, tourists, retirees, body builders, and the occasional celebrity fill the sidewalks. When the sun goes down, the street pulsates with the rhythms of its clubs and trendy bars and glows in various shades of neon.

Still, Ocean Drive's success has not come without a price. As property values rebounded, so too did the cost of housing, especially problematic for moderate- and low-income retirees. While some progress has been made by the city and nonprofit groups to increase the amount of affordable housing, a 2007 survey found that more than half of the residents think more is needed. Single-family home prices in Miami Beach in 2007 averaged $850,000.

While the final chapter of Ocean Drive's recovery has yet to be written, pages penned to date show the economic value and staying power that result when citizens, business interests, and city officials join together to protect and enhance the things that make their community unique.

South Temple Street is not just a commercial street. It includes a mixed use area with residences as well as religious, educational, recreational, office, and retail establishments. The Cathedral of the Madeleine, finished in 1909, features a Romanesque exterior and a Gothic interior.

tephdra

CHAPTER 9

South Temple Street
Salt Lake City, Utah

Intended to be the most prominent and magnificent thoroughfare in Salt Lake City, if not the state of Utah, South Temple Street has evolved over the past 150 years into a grand boulevard that reflects the bold vision of its founders. First proffered in Joseph Smith's 1833 Plat of Zion, South Temple Street was not realized until 1847 when Brigham Young and other Mormon settlers reached Salt Lake City.

This 18-block stretch of road, lined with mansions and numerous deciduous trees, including Green Ash, London Plane Trees, Honey Locust, Flowering Pear and Lavalle Hathornes, serves as a major east-west corridor. It is bounded to the west by the renovated Union Pacific Railroad Depot and, to the east, by a historic neighborhood and the University of Utah. South Temple Street boasts a variety of land uses. Predominantly commercial throughout the central business district, it transitions to a mixed-use area that, while residential in nature, includes religious, educational, recreational, office, and retail establishments.

Originally known as Brigham Boulevard, South Temple Street began as a dirt road. Through the 1860s, its agrarian landscape and architecture—small adobe homes, gardens, and barnyards—were indistinguishable from that in the rest of the city. The strategic decision by leaders of the Church of the Latter Day Saints to build their homes on South Temple presaged the street's import.

In 1924, Salt Lake City adopted a zoning ordinance to allow for the adaptive reuse of larger residences, which preserved historic houses and mitigated the need to construct new buildings.

Courtesy of the Utah State Historical Society

Originally known as Brigham Boulevard, South Temple Street was a dirt road until leaders of the Church of the Latter Day Saints built their homes there, presaging the street's importance. By 1909, the year this photo was taken, it was a popular promenade.

Analía Ferreyra Valdemoros

South Temple features mansions and numerous deciduous trees, including Green Ash, London Plane, Honey Locust, Flowering Pear and Lavalle Hathornes. Here is the sidewalk in front of the governor's mansion.

The street developed with a variation in block size on the northern and southern sides. Salt Lake City initially had one-acre blocks with four families per block. Each family's plot had a house, barn, and garden. The south side of South Temple adhered to this design, whereas the north side was platted with smaller lots. The corridor was unified, however, by its consistent streetscape. Today, the city's design guidelines for South Temple strive to reinforce these traditional development patterns.

The arrival of the railroad and, later, a mining boom brought great prosperity and changed the face of South Temple Street. Some of Utah's best-known architects—Walter Ware, Frederick Albert Hale, and Richard A. Kletting, for example—conceived grand homes, establishing a precedent for excellence in design and craftsmanship. The corridor—home to mining magnates, and religious and political leaders, including Utah's governor—features a range of architectural styles, including Victorian, Romanesque, and Classic and Renaissance Revival.

Among the prominent features of South Temple Street's homes are front porches, which help establish a human scale, and intricate architectural features and finishes. Porches often are embellished with ornamentation as are doors, windows, eaves, and gable ends. Roofs are important visual features due to the large house size. Wood and tile shingles, slate, and asphalt are common roofing materials.

South Temple Street also is home to one of the world's richest compendiums of religious and institutional buildings. Mormon and Masonic temples, Presbyterian and Catholic churches, and fraternal clubhouses line the 2.25-mile road. Apartment buildings, constructed in the 1920s and '30s, are some of the most elegant multifamily structures in Salt Lake City.

In 1924, the city adopted a zoning ordinance to allow for the adaptive reuse of larger residences. The aging and relocation of many wealthy families, coupled with the 1913 imposition of a federal income tax that eroded some families' fortunes, left a smaller pool of residents able to afford these opulent homes. By permitting commercial, retail, and educational uses in residences, the ordinance strove to preserve historic houses, to mitigate the need to construct new buildings, and to create a smoother transition from the urban core to residential neighborhoods.

During the 1960s and '70s, shifts in stylistic preferences and construction technologies produced architectural specimens that were incompatible in scale, massing, and materials with existing structures along South Temple. Many mansions were demolished to make way for contemporary buildings. This, combined with amendments to the zoning code in 1976 that encouraged commercial development and higher residential densities, resulted in the loss of significant structures.

While South Temple Street handles a lot of traffic, the street's pedestrian orientation minimizes vehicular impacts by segregating those on foot from the traffic lanes.

The deterioration of the street's historic residential character eventually caused an uproar among residents and spurred local preservation efforts. Since South Temple Street's adoption as a local historic district in 1976 and a National Historic District six years later, efforts have focused on the preservation of historic buildings, the maintenance of historic street features, and the adaptation and integration of significant historic features into today's streetscape. When the street was reconstructed in the late 1970s, existing carriage walks, sandstone retaining walls, and hitching posts were left in place. In the early 2000s, when the city embarked on a streetscape improvement project, lattice posts that were once used for streetcars were transformed into streetlamps. New sidewalks, signage, and street furniture—all in keeping with the street's historic character—were added.

Development along South Temple is covered by the Central Community Master Plan, adopted by the Salt Lake City Council in November 2005. Since 1987, the city has integrated historic preservation policies and concerns into its community master plans but now is developing a separate historic preservation plan. Zoning ordinances guide development, which is subject to design review.

South Temple was designed from inception to handle multiple modes of transportation. It has accommodated horse-drawn carriages, streetcars, trolleys, bicycles, and automobiles over the past 150 years. Like most of Salt Lake City's downtown streets, South Temple is 132 feet wide. While it handles a lot of traffic, the street's pedestrian orientation minimizes vehicular impacts by segregating those on foot from the traffic lanes. The abundance of trees, some as old as 100 years, and a generally uniform setback alignment on individual blocks create a safer, more enjoyable pedestrian experience.

Today, South Temple Street includes both bike and car lanes and, in the downtown section, two light rail stations. Parts of the street also are incorporated into several bus routes.

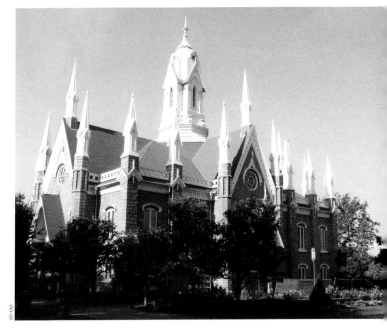

The Salt Lake Assembly Hall, owned by the Church of Jesus Christ of Latter-day Saints, was built for $90,000 in 1882 from granite discarded from the construction of Salt Lake Temple on Temple Square.

"South Temple simply tells the great story of our city's past," says Salt Lake City planner Ana Valdemoros, "and is also a statement of the efficient combination of historic preservation and modern planning tools."

While early Mormon leaders, who intended South Temple to be a prestigious boulevard, might not recognize it today, the street has fulfilled the founders' vision and taken its place among the greatest streets in America due to the ongoing commitment of city leaders, residents, and local planners.

The Beehive House was built in 1854 and served as home to Brigham Young when he was President of the Church of Jesus Christ of Latter-day Saints and governor of the Utah Territory.

The St. Charles Avenue streetcars have run since 1835, making the line the oldest, continually operating line in the world. This photo celebrates the reopening of the line, two years after it was shut down by Hurricane Katrina.

ST. CHARLES   61

915

DON'S RV DRIVING
CALL 504-3000

Please Have Exact Fare
Or RTA Pass Ready

915

#54
Judy
Bajoie-Phillips

State Representative
District 91

CHAPTER 10

St. Charles Avenue
New Orleans, Louisiana

Known as the "Jewel of America's Grand Avenues," St. Charles Avenue has served as a majestic gateway to New Orleans for nearly two centuries. While this grand boulevard resonates with the beat of modern living, the slow, steady rhythm of the past echoes through the meticulously landscaped yards of the Garden District.

Since 1835, this oak-lined avenue, an icon of Southern style and charm, has been home to the St. Charles Avenue streetcar—the oldest, continually operating line in the world. Since its inception, the streetcar line has shuttled workers between the town of Carrollton and the heart of the Crescent City—one of the most visually stunning transportation arteries in the world.

*St. Charles Avenue is home to historic Audubon Park and Loyola and Tulane universities,
but it is best known as a place of residential grandeur.*

*St. Charles Avenue was paved in
the 1880s with asphalt. The project
established asphalt as the best material for
streets. Nearly 30 years later, the avenue
was lined with palm trees.*

Whether viewed from the streetcar, which runs down the avenue's grassy median, or while walking through the heart of the Garden District, the lush, almost tropical, surroundings and elegant residences evoke a sense of romanticism. St. Charles Avenue truly is a feast for the eyes.

In the early years, the streetcars were powered by horses, mules, overhead cables, ammonia engines, and steam engines. The line was electrified in 1893. Today, streetcars that were common all over the United States in the early parts of the twentieth century still run the length of St. Charles Avenue. Most of the streetcars currently on the line are Perley Thomas cars dating from the 1920s. One 1890s vintage streetcar is still in running condition.

The streetcar line, which today carries tourists, students, shoppers, and commuters, was added to the National Register of Historic Places in 1973. As a result, the Regional Transit Authority has rejected adding air conditioning. The streetcars' double-hung windows can easily be opened to emit the cooling breezes generated by the moving cars so it's always a comfortable ride. Partially closed since hurricane Katrina, the streetcar line is expected to be fully functional in 2008.

As the streetcar line evolved—from mule power to steam to electric—so, too, did this six-mile stretch of street. Although it follows, to some degree, the curve of the Mississippi River, St. Charles Avenue is an integral part of New Orleans's rectangular street grid. The boulevard stops at the edge of the Vieux Carre, the city's historic district.

When St. Charles Avenue was paved in the 1880s, it was the largest asphalt project in the country. It also established

asphalt as the best paving material available. Soon other cities would follow New Orleans's lead.

St. Charles Avenue is home to historic Audubon Park and Loyola and Tulane universities—the city's renowned centers of higher education—and many historic churches and synagogues. But, it is best known as a place of residential grandeur. The street contains one of the most magnificent collections of antebellum Greek Revival homes, once inhabited by the city's most affluent and powerful.

Following the Civil War, the more robust Italianate style replaced Greek Revival. In the early 1870s, Queen Anne and Eastlake styles became popular, creating an eclectic group of residences in the Garden District. Despite its reputation for opulence, the district features many working class homes, predominantly double gallery and shotgun styles.

After World War II, a number of historic houses were torn down and replaced by large-scale apartment and commercial buildings. The wave of redevelopment led the city to adopt a moratorium on the demolition of older homes in 1972 while it determined whether a

*Some of the historic homes along the
avenue have been converted to hotels.
The avenue is truly multi-modal,
offering excellent opportunities for either
biking or walking to and from Audubon
Park and Tulane and Loyola universities.*

Long a source of local pride, St. Charles Avenue survives today, in part, due to its roots
in the city's cultural traditions.

historic district commission was warranted. Extensions were given over the next three years until historic district status was granted to the area. Still, much of St. Charles Avenue is unprotected, resulting in some incompatible development, including fast-food restaurants.

The boulevard's historic district runs between Jackson Avenue and Jena Street. The majority of homes along this segment of the avenue are frame constructed and set back from the front property line behind ornamental cast-iron fences. The separation of the houses from one another, and from the sidewalks, adds to the perceived width of the street and provides additional areas for landscaping.

In 1987, the city council zoned a one-mile stretch of St. Charles, between Jefferson and Broadway, RS-1A. This new zoning, the most restrictive single-family residential zoning found in the East Bank portion of the city, was designed to lower densities, achieve a greater spaciousness, and protect the historic homes in the corridor.

Local residents keep close watch on developments along St. Charles Avenue. For example, the Coliseum Square Association, a volunteer group of business owners and residents, works closely with city planners and leaders to

St. Charles Avenue is probably best known as a place of residential grandeur. The street contains one of the most magnificent collections of antebellum Greek Revival homes, once inhabited by the city's most affluent and powerful.

insure the protection of the Lower Garden District through which the avenue runs. The Garden District Association and St. Charles Avenue Association act similarly.

Neighborhood associations reacted vociferously in November 2007 to a property owner's proposal to change the zoning on his St. Charles Avenue residence, drastically reducing restrictions in order to replace a three-unit 1928 structure with a larger, more modern condominium building. Critics warned that approving the zoning change would open the door to a flood of requests that could destroy the beauty and ambiance of upper St. Charles Avenue.

After the city planning commission unanimously denied the request, the developer opted to appeal to the city council. He withdrew the appeal following the uproar and planned to consider other options that would allow the project to proceed but afford a greater level of local design review.

Long a source of local pride, St. Charles Avenue survives today, in part, due to its roots in the city's cultural traditions. It is the historic New Orleans Carnival parade route. Virtually all major parades originate in the Uptown and Mid-City districts and follow a route along St. Charles Avenue. Several homes and intersections remain integral to the festivities.

This combination of history, culture, and tradition has sustained St. Charles Avenue, setting it apart as one of America's premier residential boulevards.

The trees arching over the sidewalk and the avenue make this one of the more visually stunning transportation corridors in the U.S.

A courtyard in Chatham Village distinctly recalls its roots in the English Garden movement.

Samantha Bosshart

CHAPTER 11

Chatham Village
Pittsburgh, Pennsylvania

Aprototype of the English Garden City movement, Chatham Village remains true to its roots—a green-belted oasis that serves as a respite to the hustle and bustle of urban life. The neighborhood's 200-year-old trees, Georgian revival architecture, and strong ties among residents have contributed to Chatham Village's unique character and sense of place.

Completed in 1935, Chatham Village was built by the Buhl Foundation after Henry Buhl Jr. left $15 million to help benefit the people of Pittsburgh. At the time, substandard housing was a major issue for the city. The foundation brought together some of the greatest design professionals of the time to collaborate on a working-class, rental-housing community. Renowned planners Clarence Stein and Henry Wright were joined by architects Charles Ingham and William Boyd, and noted landscape architect Ralph Griswold.

A virtual nature preserve, Chatham Village includes a 25-acre greenbelt comprised of mature forest, pristine and uncut since colonial settlement.

Built-in garages were an innovation introduced earlier in Radburn, New Jersey. The garages in Chatham Village, however, are sited on slopes to give the perception that cars park below grade.

Pedestrians in Chatham Village can walk down heavily wooded paths marked with hedges, stone walls, and small gardens.

Tucked into a 46-acre rolling landscape considered not developable by the City of Pittsburgh, Chatham Village features 197 compact red-brick rowhouses grouped around five, large, garden courtyards. The backs of the houses face the streets and cars are kept at the periphery. The terracing of the homes into the hillsides not only respects the geography but adds visual variety to the massing and roof line of the housing. More than a third of the units have built-in garages—an innovation introduced earlier by Stein and Wright in Radburn, New Jersey. Garages are sited on slopes to give the perception from surrounding hilltops that cars park below grade.

Slender pedestrian pathways meander past perfectly clipped rows of hedges, stone walls, and pocket gardens; through archways; and up and down stone stairways. A virtual nature preserve, Chatham Village includes a 25-acre greenbelt comprised of mature forest, pristine and uncut since colonial settlement. Wooded trails, streams, footbridges, and a spring-fed waterfall co-exist with playgrounds, ball fields, tennis courts, and a picnic area.

To supplement the 200-year-old towering oaks in the greenbelt area, known as Chatham Wood, a massive planting project was undertaken in 1936. More than 2,000 tees and shrubs were transplanted. Of the 40 varieties used, most were native to Western Pennsylvania.

Chatham Hall, originally the Thomas Bingham house, serves as the neighborhood's social center. A Greek Revival mansion that dates from 1849, the home was renovated twice. In 1935 the cellar was transformed into a full basement, and a new heating system, restrooms, and hardwood floors were added. The second renovation occurred in 1992 when the kitchen was updated and the powder room was made handicap accessible.

A 19-unit apartment building was added to the neighborhood in 1956. The three-story Chatham Manor sits on the high point of the neighborhood immediately opposite the commercial buildings. It too is built in the Georgian Revival style and features a stone-trimmed entrance, flat roof, and wooden double-hung windows similar to those in the townhouses.

Although Chatham Village was constructed in three phases, the consistent application of design concepts and landscaping gives visual unity to the neighborhood. A standard building setback line was used along streets, and matching street trees and hedges helped unify the development. The neighborhood was named a National Historic Landmark District in 2005.

With two goals in mind—improving housing for moderate-income families and creating a long-term investment—the Buhl Foundation directed the architects

In designing Chatham Village, Stein and Wright were able to accommodate the car without allowing it to control human interaction.

to use permanent materials, such as brick, slate, copper, and wrought iron. A mix of unit sizes—two, three, and four bedrooms—was intended to attract a diverse group of residents. By today's standards, most units are small. A large, three-bedroom townhouse is just 1,110 square feet.

Chatham Village is best explored on foot. Because the backs of homes are oriented toward the street, little of architectural significance is visible from the curved roads that follow the contours of the hillsides. Roads form loops to prevent streets from serving as shortcuts. Speed bumps further slow local traffic.

In designing Chatham Village, Stein and Wright were able to accommodate the car without allowing it to control human interaction. Wherever possible, cars travel at a level lower than the courtyards and the first floors of the townhouses to eliminate noise and headlights. To further reduce vehicular distractions, kitchens and the service side of the houses face the streets while living rooms and front doors have a view of the courtyard. Parking for those houses without integral garages is provided in compounds, allowing for additional green space. Off-street bays provide parking for visitors. The separation of pedestrian and vehicular traffic provides an increased sense of safety and community.

Just a 25-minute walk from downtown Pittsburgh, Chatham Village is served by public transit. Buses depart regularly, and the Duquesne Incline—an operational late nineteenth century tramway that intersects bus lines—is five minutes away by foot.

Chatham Village has the distinction of being Pittsburgh's first all-gas community. All major utilities—gas, sewer, water, electricity, telephone, and cable TV—enter homes underground.

As times have changed, so too has the ownership and management of Chatham Village. During its first three decades, Chatham Village was a rental community. In 1961, when the Buhl Foundation moved on to other philanthropic endeavors, it sold the units to a resident cooperative that assumed a master mortgage backed by the federal government. For the next 20 years or so, the village functioned as a "par value" co-op with limits on the appreciation of share values. Since the mid-1980s, Chatham Village has been a market value co-op. Residents do not hold title to their homes; they own shares in the cooperative. They also pay a monthly homeowner's fee for services ranging from home and landscape maintenance to security.

As one of the purest domestic examples of a movement to ameliorate the deleterious effects of sprawl, Chatham Village, at 75 years of age, functions better than many newer incarnations of the same ideals—making it as relevant today as it was when built.

Chatham Village features 197 compact red-brick rowhouses. The backs of the houses face the streets and cars are kept at the periphery.

Five large garden courtyards make up the organizing principle for the village, providing ample open green space.

The Eastern Market from which the neighborhood takes its name has been in continuous operation since 1873. It is the sole survivor of a food-distribution system that dates to President Jefferson's efforts to improve livability in the city

andertho

CHAPTER 12

Eastern Market
Washington, D.C.

Sitting in the shadow of the U.S. Congress, the Eastern Market neighborhood of Capitol Hill has retained its unpretentious, charming nature for more than 200 years. As a result of its original design and the community's commitment to local preservation, the area has weathered many political and economic storms to emerge today as a thriving residential community with a strong sense of its history as well as its future.

Pierre L'Enfant's 1791 plan for Washington, D.C., with its wide and open avenues, circles, parks, and public squares, continues to define Eastern Market to this day. That same year, President Washington, eager to establish the seat of government on the banks of the Potomac, reached agreement with landowners, many of whom resided in what is now the Eastern Market neighborhood. The landowners conveyed, at no cost to the government, portions of their farms for streets and parks, and they sold land for government buildings at $66 per acre. The remaining land was laid out in building lots and equally apportioned between the federal government and landowners.

Eastern Market currently serves a diverse and broad cross-section of people, promotes community involvement, and operates as a hub for social activity.

In the 1970s, Eastern Market residents defeated a proposal to transform East Capitol Street into a boulevard of federal office buildings. They preserved instead beautifully colored streetscapes.

The Market hosts many regular and special activities, including art fairs, that draw visitors from all parts of the D.C. metropolitan area.

Eastern Market's first residents were craftsmen who built and repaired ships at the Washington Navy Yard, which opened in 1799. Within a decade, shops, goldsmiths and blacksmiths, and churches filled the neighborhood. Today, tree-lined residential streets—replete with nineteenth century manor houses, federal townhouses, small frame dwellings, and ornate Italianate homes—open out into pulsating commercial districts with their own eclectic mix of tenants.

While densely populated and fully developed, Eastern Market retains much of the open space visualized by L'Enfant. The neighborhood's commercial district stretches for several blocks along Pennsylvania Avenue. Populated by a mix of locally owned businesses and some franchises, the broad avenue is busy nearly round the clock. Pedestrians—many arriving by Metro rail—window shop, run errands, or grab a bite to eat.

One of the more important neighborhood structures is the Eastern Market itself, which was been in continuous operation since 1873. The sole survivor of a food-distribution system that dates to President Jefferson's efforts to improve livability in the city, the market was officially established in 1805. Architect Adolf Cluss's utilitarian structure is based

on the prevailing ideas for market design. The Italianate style adopted by Cluss for the market's South Hall made the operation of windows and doors easier for merchants and shoppers. By 1908, Eastern Market was unofficially recognized as the town center of Capitol Hill.

The market currently serves a diverse and broad cross-section of people, promotes community involvement, and operates as a hub for social activity. It easily accommodates the transportation needs of pedestrians, bicyclists, drivers, and transit users, and it meets the community need for a local market. Residents view the market as a town square of sorts,

Residents have acquired a reputation for civic activism, derailing a proposal to renovate the market for fear that modifications might compromise the building's historic character.

queuing up early on Saturday mornings for blueberry pancakes at Market Lunch, then strolling through the South Hall to purchase prime cuts of meat, seafood, poultry, and hunks of cheese. Outside, local farmers set up stands offering locally grown fruit, vegetables, cut flowers, and homemade breads and jams. It is the heart, as well as the soul, of the neighborhood.

Several attempts by the District of Columbia government to close the Eastern Market, most recently in the

features monuments to President Abraham Lincoln and Civil Rights Activist Mary McLeod Bethune. Picnics are common three seasons of the year, and the park is such a favorite of joggers that constant foot traffic has worn a dirt path along the perimeter.

The Pennsylvania Avenue corridor is home to 12 properties—such as parks, medians, and triangles—administered by the National Park Service. One of these parcels

(Left) Pedestrians—many arriving in the neighborhood by Metro rail—have a variety of activities available to them around the clock. (Below) An April 2007 fire caused businesses in the market to be temporarily relocated during rebuilding. In the meantime, citizens continued to support the market, where vendors simply set up outside until the structure could be reopened.

mid-1950s, spurred residents into action to sustain it. By the 1970s, residents had acquired a reputation for civic activism. Among their successes was the defeat of a proposal to transform East Capitol Street into a boulevard of federal office buildings and plans to erect the city's tallest high rise on Pennsylvania Avenue. In the early 1990s, a group of residents derailed a proposal to renovate the market for fear that modifications might compromise the building's historic character. Renovation plans progressed after the establishment of a citizens advisory committee in 1999.

Although an April 2007 fire caused businesses in the market to be temporarily relocated during rebuilding, citizens have demonstrated their commitment and tenacity to sustaining their special neighborhood by pressing city officials and others to create a vision and plan for permanent restoration of the 134-year-old structure.

Another significant example of the neighborhood's investment in communities of value is the Barracks Row Main Street program, an economic revitalization effort that seeks to restore small businesses and make the neighborhood more self-supporting. Barracks Row, which runs from Pennsylvania Avenue south to the Navy Yard, has emerged as a prime shopping and dining destination.

The recreation needs of Eastern Market residents are met by Lincoln Park, situated on the northeast corner of the neighborhood. The park, part of L'Enfant's plan,

is near the Eastern Market Metro station and is included in the National Capital Planning Commission's 2001 Memorials and Museums Master Plan. The plan ensures that future generations will have a sufficient supply of preeminent sites, outside of the city's monumental core, for museums and memorials.

The Eastern Market neighborhood is a thriving example of the spirit and commitment of residents. Their civic pride and dedication, combined with the centuries-old vision for this community, sustain this neighborhood's unique characteristics.

Elmwood Village evolves from Joseph Ellicott's 1804 plan for the city of Buffalo, New York. The neighborhood is marked by great architecture, a magnificent arts community, and a vibrant mix of uses.

1000words

CHAPTER 13

Elmwood Village
Buffalo, New York

Located at the crossroads of a historically significant parkway system and home to an impressive collection of world-class architecture, Elmwood Village is a premier urban, mixed-use neighborhood that dates back to Joseph Ellicott's 1804 plan for the City of Buffalo. The neighborhoods' vitality, broad spectrum of cultural and social assets, and its commitment to maintaining high community standards while solving real problems set it apart from other urban communities.

Tucked inside the city limits, Elmwood Village is a neighborhood where one can find examples of works by renowned landscape designer Frederick Law Olmsted and architect Frank Lloyd Wright. The village also is home to several world-class cultural institutions, including the Albright-Knox Art Gallery, which contains one of the country's best collections of modern art. It includes a prosperous commercial district, primarily along Elmwood Avenue, with more than 200 shops and restaurants. Four colleges and universities are located in or near the neighborhood, adding to the area's diversity and vibrancy. Helping make the neighborhood attractive and comfortable to pedestrians is the Elmwood Village Association, which has established design guidelines for the area to ensure new development does not detract from the existing architecture and character.

It was a series of planning efforts spanning two centuries that wove Elmwood Village's intricate urban, economic, and cultural tapestry.

There are three parkways designed by Frederick Law Olmsted running through the village, each of which features some fascinating residential architecture. The William Heath House was designed by Frank Lloyd Wright.

While Ellicott's plan gave definition to this neighborhood, it was a series of planning efforts spanning two centuries that wove Elmwood Village's intricate urban, economic, and cultural tapestry. The earliest, in 1868, was Frederick Law Olmsted's Park and Parkway System. Delaware Park, at the village's northeastern corner, is considered the system's crown jewel. Simply named The Park by Olmsted, this 350-acre oasis is Buffalo's equivalent to New York's Central Park. Criss-crossing the village are three of Olmsted's tree-lined parkways, each graced with the homes of nineteenth century industrial leaders and today's visionaries.

Fine examples of residential and institutional architecture abound. H.H. Richardson's Buffalo State Hospital complex and Frank Lloyd Wright's William Heath House are joined by Eliel and Eero Saarinen's modernist Kleinhan's Music

Simply named The Park by Frederick Law Olmsted, Delaware Park is a 350-acre oasis anchoring the northeast corner of the neighborhood.

Hall and E.B. Green's Greek-revival Albright Knox Art Gallery. The neighborhood boasts a variety of building styles, including Queen Anne, Second Empire, Italianate, Victorian Gothic, and French Second Empire.

Despite these assets, residents left Elmwood Village for suburbia during the latter half of the twentieth century. A dwindling customer base caused businesses along Elmwood Avenue, the community's main street, to close shop. In the 1980s and early 1990s, the street saw a slow resurgence of small, funky retailers and college bars, attracted by quirky spaces and rock-bottom rents.

To encourage an economic and cultural renaissance, the nonprofit Elmwood Village Association was formed in 1994. With membership drawn from both the business and residential sectors, the organization used planning to reclaim the neighborhood's former vitality. One of its first successes was narrowing Elmwood Avenue and widening its sidewalks to shift the street's emphasis from cars to pedestrians.

Elmwood Avenue businesses rely heavily on foot traffic, so the streetscape is of prime importance to retailers.

Elmwood Village hosts a number of world-class cultural institutions, including the Greek Revival Albright-Knox Art Gallery.

celiathepoet

Intelligent street design and management has enhanced the visibility of local shops, restaurants, and entertainment venues. Elmwood Avenue businesses rely heavily on foot traffic, so the streetscape is of prime importance to retailers. Today, Elmwood Avenue is one of Buffalo's busiest commercial districts with some 200 boutiques, restaurants, and taverns.

It also is a place where business owners and residents work together to preserve the community's unique urban character and bolster its image. The result is a lively, walkable, clean, safe, and sustainable district where community spirit is contagious.

In 2005, the City of Buffalo announced plans to reconstruct a segment of Elmwood Avenue. The village association solicited neighborhood input and presented an alternative plan with a higher level of pedestrian amenities, including intersection bulb-outs, traffic circles, and other traffic calming measures. The Elmwood Village community hopes to have many of these elements included in the city's final reconstruction plan.

Design guidelines adopted by the association have resulted in new mixed-use structures built up to the street and in character with neighborhood architectural styles rather than single-use buildings set back from the street and surrounded by parking. The association also offers grants to individual businesses and building owners to improve or reconstruct their facades in accordance with the design guidelines.

A street banner project, which received funding in mid-2007, will help the association create a new identity within Elmwood Village. The wayfinding project, designed to enhance cultural tourism, divides the village into four color-coded districts, each of which will be reflected in a new visitors guide and map. The project complements the community's branding and beautification efforts.

Elmwood Village has a long history of embracing those who are economically or socially disadvantaged. The neighborhood has been home to the Buffalo State Hospital for the Mentally Ill for more than a century. Several food pantries and soup kitchens are found here and many residents use Section 8 housing vouchers. Diversity is celebrated in the many ethnic restaurants and shops offering African goods and Asian foods.

Celebrations are not unusual in the community. The Elmwood Avenue Festival of the Arts, begun in 1999, spotlights local culture, fine art, music, dance, and theater. The two-day event attracts more than 170 "world-class"

artisans and prides itself on being earth-friendly. Garden Walk Buffalo includes stops in Elmwood Village. And, the neighborhood's summer concert series and its Tour of Kitchens draw sizable crowds.

The Elmwood-Bidwell Farmers Market operates each Saturday from mid-May to mid-November. It is a producer-only market, meaning that vendors grow or produce what they sell themselves; reselling is not allowed.

Standards are high in Elmwood Village, but given its proactive, "can-do" attitude, the neighborhood is able to support the needs of today's local businesses and residents without losing sight of its historic past.

Justin Azzarella

Elmwood Avenue anchors the neighborhood with one of the busiest commercial districts in the city. It is home to nearly 200 boutiques, restaurants, and taverns.

A great strength of the First Addition neighborhood in Lake Oswego, Oregon, a suburb of Portland, is that most everything one would need, including a multi-use downtown, is within walking distance.

Denis Egner

CHAPTER 14

First Addition
Lake Oswego, Oregon

Asmall-town atmosphere, where everything is within walking distance, and residents committed to preserving their town's quality of life have combined to make the First Addition neighborhood in Lake Oswego one of Portland's most desirable bedroom communities.

Initially platted in 1888 by the Oregon Iron and Steel Company for its workers, First Addition has the character and feel of a more rural place. The neighborhood is home to a collection of unpretentious and eclectic houses, some dating to the late nineteenth century. Despite the city's hilly landscape, First Addition is relatively level and laid out on a grid where the north-south roads are identified by numbers—First Street, Second Street, etc.—and east-west connectors with letters—A Avenue, B Avenue, etc. Some 1,700 people currently reside in this 120-acre community.

First Addition is a cohesive artifact of the era and circumstances from which it sprang—the need to house iron workers. Gothic, Prairie Tudor, Craftsman, bungalow, and ranch are among the single-family housing styles. Residential blocks, divided lengthwise by 20-foot alleys, provide rear access to homes for off-street parking and trash removal.

Small-scale, residential streets with minimal paved areas and vegetative canopies provide interesting routes to myriad destinations and promote neighborly interaction.

First Addition is a strict grid, arranged by numbered and lettered streets. Here is C Street in a historic photo.

The Lake Oswego farmers market is a central gathering place for all Lake Oswego citizens, including residents of First Addition.

To protect the neighborhood's existing character and style, residents have worked with municipal officials to adopt design guidelines for new development and residential additions. Lot coverage and floor area ratios incorporate design proportionality. Front porches, covering at least half the house width, are required on all new dwellings and roof pitch must be at least 6:12; no shed or flat roofs are permitted.

Despite the design guidelines, residential demolitions increased over the past few years during a particularly hot real estate market, and the neighborhood lost more than 20 homes. To stem further teardowns, the City of Lake Oswego is reviewing its base zone and infill design review standards.

The neighborhood also supports multifamily, duplex, and accessory dwelling units. Many of the multifamily structures are located in the East End where allowable densities are higher. A recently approved condominium development in this commercial district is 60 units per acre.

Compact enough that the neighborhood can be traversed end-to-end on foot, First Addition has its own grocery store, adult community center, and library. There also is a post office, police and fire stations, three churches, and a mixed-use retail, commercial, and service area nearby.

Mixed-use development has become increasingly popular in the East End Commercial District.

To maintain the pedestrian-friendly street design in the area, the city's redevelopment agency offers façade grants for existing retail and capital improvement projects. In 2002, such a project along First Street reinforced the corridor's pedestrian orientation through the use of brick-paved sidewalks, and installation of basalt seat walls and a street clock.

First Addition views its roads as more than connectors. They are places unto themselves. Small-scale, residential streets with minimal paved areas and vegetative canopies provide interesting routes to myriad destinations and promote neighborly interaction. Traffic calming strategies, including roundabouts, discourage through-traffic.

Safety, aesthetic, and environmental enhancements are at the heart of the redesign of Tenth Street, the neighborhood's western boundary. The five-block project will provide a safe route to school for children, slow traffic, and create a unique and attractive gateway that welcomes residents and visitor.

Also along Tenth Street the city is taking the community's environmental values a step further by implementing a surface water project to slow and treat stormwater within the right-of-way. The recipient of more than 40 inches of rain each year, Lake Oswego has made green streets a priority. The Tenth Street project includes 19 water-quality planters with cascading water features along with new landscaping. Impervious surfaces will be reduced, curbs eliminated, and permeable pavers installed.

What First Addition lacks in terms of architectural magnificence and splendor it makes up with physical beauty and a striking array of flora.

What First Addition lacks in terms of architectural magnificence and splendor it makes up with physical beauty and a striking array of flora. Homeowners' plantings stand next to tall deciduous and evergreen trees. Trees are so important that the neighborhood plan includes a "distinctive natural area trees" inventory, a Garden Club Tree Walk (with stops to view 18 trees, among them a 100-year-old sequoia), a tree removal and protection code, and a designation program for historically significant trees.

The real outdoor jewel of the neighborhood is Tryon Creek State Park whose canyons and ravines form a dramatic backdrop and inviting retreat to the neighborhood's north. This 645-acre natural area features eight miles of hiking trails and opportunities for fishing and wildlife observation. Centrally located Rossman Park serves as a neighborhood gathering place. Its playground equipment and picnicking area allows for both passive and active uses.

Within walking distance of First Addition are two other parks—Millennium Plaza and Foothills—that offer options for recreation and entertainment. Both feature outdoor concerts throughout the summer, and Millennium Plaza Park hosts a weekly Farmers Market from May through October.

To ensure the continuation of First Addition's worth and charm, residents enacted a plan that provides customized guidance on land use, building site design, and capital improvements. Developed more than 11 years ago, the community's plan is intended to help retain those aspects of the neighborhood that contribute to its quality of life: housing variety and affordability, small-town atmosphere, pedestrian-friendly streets and alleys, and access to commerce and transit.

Paul Espe

First Addition was built to house iron workers and is marked by a number of residential styles, including Gothic, Prairie Tudor, Craftsman, ranch, and bungalow houses. This Colonial Revival bungalow dates from 1925.

Lake Oswego's public transit center, located within the boundaries of First Addition, is served by four bus lines. The primary feeder bus is Line 35, which shuttles commuters to downtown Portland. The addition of a street car is under consideration as both a commuter transit option and local downtown circulator.

Thoroughly vernacular in its origins, plan, and housing stock, this great neighborhood shows how residents, through cooperation and persistence, have capitalized on the area's underlying value.

An attractive streetscape provides safe pedestrian access to public transportation facilities and local stores.

Paul Espe

Hillcrest is one of San Diego's most diverse neighborhoods, marked by colorful and eclectic architecture that creates a unique sense of place.

Allan Ferguson

CHAPTER 15

Hillcrest
San Diego, California

One of the country's more resilient neighborhoods, Hillcrest has, nonetheless, been shaped by the country's economic cycles, demographic changes, and periods of growth, decline, and resurgence. But its unique blend of topography, architecture, and residents has made this neighborhood a trendsetter and catalyst for change.

Nestled in the heart of San Diego's Uptown District, Hillcrest overlooks San Diego Bay. The neighborhood's southern border is adjacent to world famous Balboa Park and the San Diego Zoo. San Diego's juxtaposition of mountains, mesas, valleys, canyons, coastal bluffs, and sandy beaches contributes to Hillcrest's distinct physical character, writes planning professor and author Gene Bunnell in *Making Places Special*. The Mediterraneanlike climate, ocean views and breezes, lush vegetation, valleys, and canyons combine with the trendy bars, restaurants, shops, salons, and spas to create a unique sense of place.

*Considered San Diego's most diverse, vibrant, and urbane neighborhood, Hillcrest has been
a source of social, cultural, and political influence.*

San Diego Historical Society

*Since its beginnings in 1907, Hillcrest
has been home to the progressive
residential designs of architect Irving
Gill, who was heavily influenced by
the Arts and Crafts movement, as well
as the works of Hazel Waterman and
Lillian Rice, two of the first women to
practice architecture in the U.S. Here
is University Ave at 6th Street in the
early twentieth century.*

It was here, in 1990, that a closed Sears store became one of the country's first compact, pedestrian-oriented, mixed-use redevelopments. Featuring some 200,000 square feet of space, the center attracted national attention as a model smart growth reuse project in which a low-density, obsolete suburban site is redeveloped for higher-density uses.

Considered San Diego's most diverse, vibrant, and urbane neighborhood, Hillcrest has been a source of social, cultural, and political influence, especially within the gay and lesbian community. Since its beginnings in 1907, the neighborhood has been a place where experimental ideas and practices have taken hold. For instance, Hillcrest is where the progressive residential designs of architect Irving Gill, who was heavily influenced by the Arts and Crafts movement, were built in the early twentieth century. The neighborhood also features works by Hazel Waterman and Lillian Rice, two of the first women to practice architecture in the U.S.

From the Mediterranean Revival style of Mercy College of Nursing to its Craftsman, Art Deco, and Moderne homes, Hillcrest historically has been known for having some of the area's more affordable housing. It also has a high percentage of single-occupancy bungalow courts, cottages, and smaller single-unit family homes, an important factor in the neighborhood's 1980's revival.

During the two preceding decades of economic stagnation, which followed the opening of a nearby shopping center, Hillcrest struggled to find its identity. To many, it was nothing more than a community of elderly and low-income residents living in run-down housing.

It was the neighborhood's occupation by elderly residents, which implied that the neighborhood was a safe one, combined with its smaller homes, which were perfect for individuals or couples, that attracted gays and lesbians to Hillcrest. Today the neighborhood is the center of San Diego's gay community. The city's annual two-day Pride Festival, which includes a parade through Hillcrest, attracts some 150,000 spectators to the downtown and 40,000 participants to nearby Balboa Park.

*The Hillcrest sign
was erected in
1940 as a gateway
and historic
landmark. It was
restored in 1977
and rebuilt a
decade later.*

Mary Wright

*Streetscape improvements in Hillcrest are funded by the Uptown Partnership,
which manages the Uptown Community Parking District.*

San Diego's annual two-day Pride Festival includes a parade through Hillcrest and attracts some 150,000 spectators to the downtown and 40,000 participants to nearby Balboa Park.

Hillcrest has a strong history of community activism. Many residents participate in the Uptown Planners Community Planning Group that advises city staff, the planning commission, and city council on development issues. The Uptown Planners, founded in 1971, reviews all proposed, discretionary development projects in the area.

The planning group presently is involved in a controversy to change building height limits along Hillcrest's transit corridors. The group, along with the Hillcrest Town Council, supports an interim, 65-foot height limit that would remain in effect until the update of the 20-year-old *Uptown Community Plan*, which was expected to begin in January 2008, is completed.

Recently proposed condominium developments triggered debate over higher-density development. While the condos fit the type of smart-growth development envisioned by the *City of Villages* plan for the corridor, residents are concerned that taller buildings will detract from the community's character and worsen traffic. Hillcrest is currently served by the San Diego bus system.

Hillcrest activism was apparent when residents sought to rebuild the Vermont Street pedestrian bridge across Washington Street in 1995. Highway officials closed the termite-damaged bridge, which connected Hillcrest's shops with University Heights, in 1979 and refused to replace it because it was not part of a highway or motor vehicle improvement project.

Residents refused to acquiesce. The community turned to the San Diego Commission for Arts and Culture for funds to build a new concrete and cobalt-blue steel pedestrian bridge as a "work of public art." The successful strategy

led the city to reconsider its approach to pedestrians. As a result, San Diego now has a separate *Pedestrian Master Plan* that guides and prioritizes scores of projects and improvements for walkers throughout the city.

Local businesses play an active role in Hillcrest. In 1921, a handful of retailers formed the Hillcrest Association. Over the next three decades, membership increased to 160. In 1984, following a two-year effort, the San Diego City Council established the city's first business improvement district (BID) in Hillcrest. Membership skyrocketed and now surpasses 1,200.

There's no mistaking Hillcrest's downtown. In 1940, the lighted "HILLCREST" sign was erected at the intersection of University and Fifth Avenues as a gateway of sorts. Restored in 1977 and rebuilt a decade later, the sign is a neighborhood landmark.

Streetscape improvements in downtown Hillcrest are partially funded by the Uptown Partnership, a nonprofit that manages the Uptown Community Parking District. From 2005–06, the partnership, working with the city and the Hillcrest Association, used $30,000 in parking funds to help reconstruct sidewalks, curbs, and pedestrian crossings along the south side of the 1200 and 1400 blocks of University Avenue. The organization has contributed to the public outreach element of the Hillcrest Corridor Mobility Plan, which is focusing on transportation-related issues along a 25-block corridor that encompasses Fourth, Fifth, and Sixth Streets from downtown San Diego to downtown Hillcrest.

Having marked the neighborhood's centennial anniversary in 2007, Hillcrest residents have much to celebrate—a community with a rich history of accomplishments and a future that looks just as promising.

The San Diego City Council established the city's first business improvement district (BID) in Hillcrest in 1984. Membership now surpasses 1,200.

North Beach, despite having an international reputation, is really a traditional neighborhood only a square mile in area. It is ethnically diverse as well as home to a number of music and art festivals and landmarks. Here are Sts. Peter and Paul Church and Russian Hill.

CHAPTER 16

North Beach
San Francisco, California

This thriving, European-style neighborhood—nestled in a sunny, wind-protected valley between San Francisco's financial district, Chinatown, and Russian and Telegraph Hills—has evolved into one of the city's most unique and authentic communities. North Beach, with the help of planning and zoning tools, has managed to preserve its essential character: a mix of tolerance and tradition in both its built and social environments.

North Beach attained international repute in the 1950s as the neighborhood in which the Beat Generation experienced its genesis. While it remains a popular pilgrimage destination for former beatniks, the neighborhood is anything but a relic. Its polyglot character and eclectic mix of mom-and-pop shops and nightclubs make it a favorite among residents and tourists alike.

North Beach is, in many ways, a traditional neighborhood. It's rarely more than a few blocks walk to find a grocery store, bakery, barber shop, hardware store, church, school, or park. What cannot be found in the neighborhood are chain stores and fast-food outlets. And that's by design.

North Beach placed controls on the type and scale of commercial uses to promote homegrown businesses and discourage chains and franchises.

In the late nineteenth century, North Beach became the neighborhood home for Irish, German, and French immigrants. By the mid-twentieth century, more than 60,000 Italians had moved here, earning it the nickname of Little Italy. This is a view of Columbus Avenue in the 1920s.

As early as the 1980s, the city placed controls on the type and scale of commercial uses as a way to help protect North Beach's identity. The idea was to promote homegrown businesses and discourage chains and franchises by including in local regulations descriptions of how North Beach businesses could operate. Small storefront sizes limit the neighborhood's appeal among corporate entities. To further dissuade chain stores, the San Francisco Board of Supervisors voted in 2005 to ban retailers with more than 11 stores from locating in the neighborhood. Potential encroachment into North Beach from businesses in the nearby financial district was fended off in 1985 by development of a new downtown plan.

Transit rich and parking poor, North Beach is a pedestrian's dream. Tourists arrive by bus or cable car and explore the neighborhood on foot. Residents use transit or bike lanes to commute. The neighborhood's main street, Columbus Avenue, connects North Beach with Fisherman's Wharf to the northwest and Chinatown and Jackson Park to the southeast. It provides clearly defined lanes for cars, cable cars, bicycles, and buses.

In mid-2007, the San Francisco County Transportation Authority embarked on a planning process to identify transportation improvements that will support livability and vitality on Columbus Avenue for residents, merchants, and tourists by enhancing pedestrian safety and traffic flow. Other changes under consideration involve streetscape improvements, intersection treatments, and open space.

Limiting car use has paid dividends in North Beach. The result has been less land for parking and more for affordable housing. And greenhouse gas emissions in North Beach are comparatively lower than those from adjacent neighborhoods.

North Beach's identity and namesake date back to the mid-nineteenth century before a finger of the San Francisco Bay that reached the neighborhood was filled. Settled in the 1850s by middle-class Americans, some 30 years later came an influx of immigrants, two-thirds of whom were mostly from Ireland, Germany, and France. By 1939, more than 60,000 Italians had moved to this square-mile neighborhood, earning it the nickname of Little Italy. The

North Beach has nearly 90 households per residential acre, making it San Francisco's densest neighborhood.

Transit rich and parking poor, North Beach is a pedestrian's dream. Tourists arrive by bus or cable car and explore the neighborhood on foot.

streets were lined with Italian restaurants, shops, and social clubs. Tourists frequented the area, drawn by the quality and affordability of the local cuisine.

With the 1950s came an influx of beatniks who filled jazz clubs, coffee houses, and esoteric bookstores. Night-clubs along Broadway hosted top entertainers. Today you can find boutique shops and restaurants mixed in with dance clubs and risque venues, making North Beach a neighborhood of contrasts and one of the liveliest parts of town.

As Chinatown became overcrowded in the 1970s, residents moved into nearby North Beach. Recognizing that an expanded Chinatown might not be as economically viable as two distinct ethnic districts, the North Beach Chamber of Commerce worked to bolster existing Italian businesses as well as to encourage new ones. Today, while Italians comprise just 15 percent of residents, Italian businesses represent about 80 percent of the neighborhood's commercial enterprises. The neighborhood hosts an Italian Heritage Parade each October.

Part of North Beach's appeal stems from restrictions on building heights and billboards. These restrictions were initiated by neighborhood associations and implemented in the 1980s. Today, historic landmarks such as Coit Tower are visible; no skyscrapers block the view. Washington Square, the neighborhood's central open space, is a place for morning Tai Chi classes, dog walking, sky gazing, and several annual festivals.

Due to its central location, North Beach is one of San Francisco's most dense neighborhoods. With some 90 households per residential acre, North Beach's density is greater than that of Russian Hill, with 50 households, and Fisherman's Wharf at 65. The number of employees per acre, 43 in North Beach, also is higher than the 24 for Russian Hill and 31 for Fisherman's Wharf.

Affordability—both residential and commercial—remains an issue in North Beach. Roughly 60 percent of the housing stock is rent controlled. An inclusionary housing program requires that new developments set aside a percentage of units as affordable. For example, the 341-unit North Beach Place apartments, which replaced crumbling 1950s mid-rises, opened to acclaim in 2004. This mixed-use project contains 34,000 feet of street-level retail and a mix of residential units: public housing, low- and moderate-income, and senior citizen. At the center of the two-block complex is a cable car turnaround, providing a convenient public transit option to residents.

What truly makes North Beach unique are the people who live there. If they were to be left behind by the market, so, too, would be the character that a century of effort has kept in place.

Yuteng Guo

(Above) Columbus Avenue, which connects North Beach with Fisherman's Wharf, Chinatown, and Jackson Park, provides clearly defined lanes for cars, cable cars, bicycles, and buses. (Below) North Beach is also home to the famous City Lights Bookstore, founded in 1953 by poet Lawrence Ferlinghetti. It published Allen Ginsberg's Howl and Other Poems.

bakkalooka

The Old West Austin Association, a neighborhood group, has been directly involved in Old West Austin's development since the early 1980s. Preservation of the area's beautiful homes has been one of its main focuses, leading to a "McMansion" ordinance to prevent inappropriate development on the neighborhood's small lots.

Chris Schorre

CHAPTER 17

Old West Austin
Austin, Texas

History, diversity, and one of the oldest oak trees in the state help distinguish Old West Austin, the most dense and diverse neighborhood in the Lone Star State's capital city. The neighborhood's character has remained largely intact due to the voluntary efforts of residents and developers in the absence of local ordinances governing building size or style.

Located west of downtown Austin and north of Lady Bird Lake, Old West Austin comprises a number of plats that were purchased and subdivided starting in 1841, two years after Austin was incorporated. The neighborhood includes several historic districts on the National Register of Historic Places. The history of the Clarksville district traces back to the 1860s when Texas Governor Elisha Pease sold some of his plantation to slaves who built homes there. A decade later Charles Clark, a freed slave, started the community named in his honor.

The Old West Austin Neighborhood Association has been instrumental in promoting mixed-use development and discouraging overbuilding on residential lots.

One of the oldest oak trees in Texas, the Treaty Oak, is in Old West Austin. Its name is derived from its history: it once was part of a stand of 14 oaks where the Comanche and Tonkawa Native American tribes held sacred meetings.

The Enfield subdivision, also in the neighborhood, was part of a 320-acre land grant by the Republic of Texas in 1841. The Old West Austin and Westline districts are also on the National Register and included in the neighborhood's boundaries.

Large shade trees and front porches lure people outside, inviting leisurely strolls and casual chats with neighbors. One of the city's oldest trees, the 600-year-old Treaty Oak, is found in Old West Austin.

A strong desire to preserve the neighborhood's roots—both physical and cultural—led residents to participate in the planning and development of the community. Its proximity to downtown, a major source of new develop-

ment, was the catalyst for resident involvement. The Old West Austin Neighborhood Association stemmed from a desire to retain the existing character of the area, which is composed mostly of single-family residences.

There are some apartments, duplexes, and student housing in Old West Austin. In fact, the University of Texas houses graduate students and their families here, contributing greatly to the diversity of the local population. Some 40 nationalities are represented at the neighborhood elementary school.

The neighborhood's retail and commercial area is dominated by locally owned businesses, including Nau Enfield Drug. With wooden, church pew-style booths, mint-green tabletops, curved soda bar and swivel stools, the pharmacy feels like it must have when the Nau brothers opened it in 1951.

Many local business owners live in Old West Austin. The neighborhood's compact commercial center consists of mostly homegrown businesses, and national chain stores are virtually nonexistent. One exception is the flagship store of the natural foods grocery chain, Whole Foods. Shops, restaurants, schools, and community centers serve as pedestrian destinations. New sidewalks and improved street lighting were recently secured through the state's Safe Route to School program and Austin's Capital Improvements Program.

The Old West Austin Neighborhood Association has been instrumental in promoting mixed-use development and discouraging overbuilding on residential lots. In the early 1980s, the organization persuaded the mayor to declare a moratorium on new multifamily construction pending the outcome of a wastewater system capacity study. Following system upgrades, a few condominiums were built. The end result, however, was the preservation of the existing housing stock, particularly bungalows and historic homes.

Old West Austin's diverse residential architectural styles are enhanced by canopies formed by the limbs of oak, elm, and pecan trees.

Old West Austin's sustainability is enhanced by small lots on narrow streets that encourage walking; front porches that take advantage of the breeze; canopies formed by shade trees; and access to public transportation.

Still, preservation continues to be a contentious issue in Old West Austin. Many neighborhood buildings and districts have been placed on the National Register, but that carries little weight when it comes to property additions or changes. In 2004, Austin authorized the establishment of local historic designations. The ordinance was amended in 2006 to include design standards for remodeling and new construction. It also raised the bar for evaluating the demolition or relocation of historic homes.

A segment of Harthan Street in Old West Austin was the first to be approved for local designation by the historic landmarks commission and planning commission. At the end of 2007, the application was awaiting action by the city council. Other nominations in the pipeline include Clarksville, which is on the National Register. In the meantime, some property owners have vowed to fight the revised ordinance.

The Old West Austin Association has been a major player in the planning of Old West Austin since developing the neighborhood's first plan in the early 1980s. As a result, developers meet with neighborhood representatives in the early stages of a proposed project. This enables residents to negotiate the inclusion of items, such as affordable housing, into mixed-use projects.

To prevent overbuilding on Old West Austin's small residential lots, generally between 6,000 and 7,000 square feet, the city adopted a "McMansion" ordinance. More moderate housing has helped curb escalating home prices.

Old West Austin boasts an interesting mix of residential and institutional architecture. Architect-designed dwellings coexist with more modest vernacular dwellings, and the collection includes period revival residences, bungalows, cottages, and apartments.

As a result of its unique Victorian Gothic architecture, the Texas Military Institute (TMI), built in 1869 on West 11th Street, is often referred to as The Castle. Homes around the property house the school's faculty. Their materials, massing, and architecture clearly associate them with TMI. The Castle and two faculty homes are designated Austin landmarks.

A Moonlight Tower, one of the city's 17 lighting towers that stand 150 feet tall and date back to 1894, still stands in the neighborhood. The tower, restored by the city in the mid 1990s, has been turned off only three times since its installation.

Old West Austin's sustainability is enhanced by several of the neighborhood's inherent characteristics: small lots on narrow streets that encourage walking; front porches that take advantage of the breeze; canopies formed by shady oak, elm, and pecan trees; and access to public transportation. These and other features show what is possible when diverse and engaged residents join together to protect and enhance what makes their neighborhood unique.

Chris Schorre

(Above) People in Old West Austin can walk to shops, restaurants, schools, and community centers. New sidewalks and improved street lighting were recently secured through the state's Safe Route to School program and Austin's Capital Improvements Program. (Below) The Texas Military Institute (TMI), built in 1869, is often referred to as The Castle. It is an Austin historic landmark.

nikkorsnapper

Park Slope provides "a living illustration of the 19th century characterization of Brooklyn as 'a city of homes and churches'." Here is a view of the corner of 6th Avenue and Carroll Street, with St. Francis Xavier Catholic Church in the background.

Olivia Klose

CHAPTER 18

Park Slope
Brooklyn, New York

There's a little bit of everything in Park Slope—stately brownstones, distinctive apartment buildings, a food co-op, a farmer's market, restaurants, shops, transit, and an adjoining park from which the neighborhood takes its name. A testament to the value of economic, architectural, and cultural diversity, this resurgent Brooklyn neighborhood is the beneficiary of active, involved residents and organizations that have worked to preserve and build upon the neighborhood's social and physical strengths.

Park Slope's architecture has changed little over the past 100 years. The neighborhood "retains an aura of the past to an extent which is unusual in New York," noted the city's Landmarks Preservation Commission in 1973 when it designated the 24-block Park Slope Historic District. "Wide sunny avenues and tree-lined streets, with houses of relatively uniform height punctuated by church spires, provide a living illustration of the 19th century characterization of Brooklyn as 'a city of homes and churches'."

"No neighborhood in America has a finer and more intact collection of late 19th-century row houses than Park Slope."

The distinctive brownstones of Park Slope.

"No neighborhood in America has a finer and more intact collection of late 19th-century row houses than Park Slope," noted architectural historian and Columbia University professor Andrew Dolkart. "Block after block is virtually unaltered, with houses ranging from grand townhouses designed by Brooklyn's leading architects, to long rows of vernacular speculator-built housing designed by the obscure architects who provided character to so many urban neighborhoods."

Park Slope's history and development is closely related to that of Prospect Park, which was dedicated in 1873. Designed by Frederick Law Olmsted and Calvert Vaux, the 585-acre park sits at the neighborhood's eastern edge. The Grand Army Plaza, with its formal garden and striking Civil War Memorial Arch, serves as a transition from Park Slope's active urban landscape to the expansive oasis.

Built on the western slope of Prospect Park, the neighborhood developed in tiers. A virtual "gold coast" of mansions—Victorian, Queen Anne, Renaissance Revival, and Romanesque—was built at the park's edge. Over time, more modest, middle- and working-class homes were constructed further down the slope. Development accelerated in 1883 following the opening of a cable railway across the Brooklyn Bridge into Manhattan.

Today, the neighborhood is bounded by Flatbush Avenue on the north, Fifth Avenue on the west, and, to the south, 15th Street. Dramatically sited at the confluence of Flatbush Avenue and Eastern Parkway is the main branch of the Brooklyn Public Library. Around the corner is the Brooklyn Museum, which sits adjacent to the 52-acre Brooklyn Botanic Garden.

Despite the neighborhood's outstanding amenities and singular quality of architecture, Park Slope suffered from disinvestment and decline during the decades following World War II. Many grand four- and five-story single-family homes of the Victorian era fell into disrepair or were chopped into rooming houses and small apartments.

The start of a decades-long turnaround began in the 1960s when visionary residents, among them Evelyn and Everett Ortner, moved into the neighborhood. The Ortners, who purchased an 1886 brownstone on Berkeley Place, became famous as two of the neighborhood's strongest advocates, encouraging friends to move there, fighting urban renewal projects that subsidized brownstone demolition, and campaigning against mortgage redlining by area banks. In 1968, the Ortners helped found what

The Grand Army Plaza sits between Park Slope and Prospect Park, providing a transition from the highly urban neighborhood to the open spaces of the 585-acre park.

is now known as the Brownstone Revival Committee, a citywide preservation group.

With Park Slope's resurgence came the displacement of lower-income and working-class families. To help retain the neighborhood's economic and social diversity, the Fifth Avenue Committee was created. The nonprofit's mission is to advance social and economic justice principally by developing and managing affordable housing and community facilities. Since its inception in 1978, the Fifth Av-

Since the opening of the Brooklyn Bridge cable railway, the number of accessible public transportation options has grown. Today Park Slope is served by numerous bus routes and train lines.

its inception in 1978, the Fifth Avenue Committee has built more than 600 affordable units, much of it in Park Slope.

Today, it is not uncommon to find families with upper, middle, and lower incomes residing on the same block. This phenomenon, far from natural, is the result of community planning and activism.

The partial rezoning of Park Slope in 2003 was designed to preserve the neighborhood's brownstones while encouraging the development of multifamily housing in selected areas. This was achieved by capping building heights on streets with brownstones while permitting taller residential structures along the Fourth Avenue transit corridor. A maximum of 12 stories is permitted under the new zoning. To allow the flow of light and air, new apartment and condominium buildings may rise in a street wall up to eight floors after

area. This once decrepit, crime-laden boulevard is now the center of local nightlife, filled with chic eateries, trendy wine bars, and an eclectic assortment of boutiques. *Zagat's* now includes many top-rated Fifth Avenue restaurants.

Park Slope's popularity has its roots in accessible public transportation. Since the opening of the Brooklyn Bridge cable railway, the number of options has grown. Today the neighborhood is served by numerous bus routes and train lines. Pedestrians, joggers, and bikers enjoy the tree-lined streets and nearby Prospect Park.

Historic in design and modern in amenities, the livability of Brooklyn's Park Slope is no hyperbole. Its architectural, recreational, transportation, and community assets all combine to make it a great community of lasting value.

The Montauk Club has been a private club since it was founded in 1889. It was designed by the famed New York architect Francis H. Kimball, who was inspired by a palace on Venice's Grand Canal. Today, the Club is a vibrant part of the neighborhood, serving as headquarters for the neighborhood association.

Prospect Park, from which the neighborhood derives its name, sits just east of Park Slope. It provides much-needed open space and even a splash of cool water on a hot day from one of its fountains.

which a setback is required to accommodate an additional four stories. The zoning change has resulted in thousands of additional housing units in Park Slope. While virtually none of it qualifies as affordable, it is a less-costly alternative to the neighborhood's mansions and brownstones.

One street over, on Fifth Avenue, a renaissance of sorts is underway. In the late 1970s, this street suffered from widespread abandonment and blight. More than 200 vacant buildings and 150 vacant lots existed within a one-mile

Situated on a bluff overlooking Elliott Bay, the
Pike Place Market neighborhood offers many
residents lovely water views.

CHAPTER 19

Pike Place Market
Seattle, Washington

Located in downtown Seattle, the Pike Place Market neighborhood encompasses roughly nine acres. Here, those living in upscale condos with views of Elliott Bay mix and mingle with occupants of five subsidized apartment buildings that are part of the historic Pike Place Market neighborhood. The market also houses four social service agencies: a health clinic, food bank, and senior and child-care centers.

With a history as rich and colorful as the produce it sells, the Pike Place Market is Seattle's most compact, walkable, and diverse neighborhood. It is functional, livable, and replete with memorable characteristics.

Pedestrians rule in the market neighborhood. They have the right of way and, when sidewalks are full, walk without fear down the middle of the street. Those choosing to drive must be willing to creep at a pedestrian pace.

A stroll down the market's main cobblestone street reveals human-scale building facades that encourage foot traffic. The rhythms of local street musicians add a sense of festivity and encourage passersby to pause and enjoy the melodies, if only for a few moments.

To preserve the market's original intent of "meet the producer," owner-operated businesses are required, and franchises and chains are not allowed.

Courtesy Seattle Municipal Archives

(Left) Pike Place Market might not exist today where it not for a revolt about the price of onions, which increased tenfold between 1906 and 1907. Outraged citizens demanded change, and a city councilman proposed a public street market. The rest is history, as they say. (Below) Steinbrueck Park, adjacent to the market's north end, serves as a gateway from the neighborhood into downtown Seattle. It is named after one of the people who fought successfully against the redevelopment of the market into high rises and parking garages in the 1960s.

Situated on a bluff overlooking Elliott Bay, the market offers many residents lovely water views. The Seattle waterfront lies directly below the neighborhood. And Steinbrueck Park, adjacent to the market's north end, serves as a gateway from the neighborhood into downtown Seattle.

The character of the neighborhood—a designated historic district since 1971—is protected by the Pike Place Market Historical Commission, which reviews all design and use requests. To preserve the market's original intent of "meet the producer," owner-operated businesses are required, and franchises and chains are not allowed. The exceptions are Starbucks and Sur la Table, as the market was home to their first stores.

Were it not for a revolt over the price of onions, the centerpiece of Seattle's Pike Place Market neighborhood might not exist today. Between 1906 and 1907, as the cost of onions increased tenfold, outraged citizens became fed up with price-gouging middlemen and demanded change. A city councilman proposed a public street market where residents could buy directly from farmers. On a dreary, damp August morning in 1907, thousands of eager shoppers quickly overwhelmed the eight farmers who set up their wagons on a boardwalk adjacent to the Leland Hotel. The first building at the market opened later that year.

Long a haven for immigrant merchants and their families, the market is a melting pot of accents, ideas, flavors, and customs. In the 1930s, the market's neon-lit clock served as the equivalent of London's Speaker's Corner with Socialists, Communists, and people from all walks of life addressing the throngs of residents and shoppers. Today the clock remains a popular meeting place, but the public expression of ideas, quiet protests, and demonstrations takes place at Steinbrueck Park.

Lydia Heard

Spared from the wrecking ball numerous times by citizen activists, Pike Place Market occupies a unique spot in Seattle's history. With the rise of the automobile in the 1920s, the city considered moving the market to allow cars easy access to the waterfront. Farmers won the fight by one council vote. A few years later, the city eyed the property for creation of a new civic building. It was the Great Depression, however, that finally brought a truce as the market became a major supplier of affordable food.

Today, Pike Place Market is recognized as the nation's premier farmers market. It is home to nearly 220 year-round commercial businesses, 210 crafters, 100 farmers, and 250 street performers. An integral part of local

The Pike Place Market neighborhood's compact, pedestrian-oriented design and range of housing options served as the inspiration for the city's Downtown Livability Plan, passed in 2006.

Pedestrians have the right of way in the neighborhood and will walk down the middle of the street when sidewalks are full.

sustainable agriculture efforts, the market attracts some 10 million visitors each year. Some come for the ethnic and specialty goods exclusive to the market, others for daily groceries.

The greatest threat to the market came after the successful 1962 World's Fair jump-started interest in the city's revitalization. The next year, an association of downtown businesses proposed replacing the market with parking garages and high-rise office buildings. The Pike Plaza Redevelopment project was submitted in Seattle's 1964 request for federal urban renewal funds.

Led by a prominent local architect and professor, Victor Steinbrueck, and artist Mark Tobey, Friends of the Market fought the city's plans. The battle raged for more than a half-dozen years and was feared lost in 1968 when the city tore down the old Armory building, now the site of Steinbrueck Park.

Preservationists ultimately prevailed and, in 1971, voters approved an initiative creating a seven-acre historic district and the Pike Place Market Historical Commission. The city then purchased most of the buildings in the district and transferred them to a newly created entity, the Pike Place Market Preservation and Development Authority.

A decade later, the authority used urban renewal money allocated to Seattle to purchase and renovate the Market District. Emphasis was placed on historic preservation of the buildings and traditional market uses. Today, within the market's historic district, nearly 500 low-income people,

most of them seniors, live in 348 residential units spread throughout eight buildings.

The market's mascot, a large bronze pig named Rachel, is more than a renowned landmark. It also is a piggybank. Rachel's proceeds—roughly $9,000 annually—support the market's social services. Locals have made a habit of emptying their pockets and rubbing Rachel's snout as they pass by.

The Pike Place Market neighborhood continues to lead by example. Its compact, pedestrian-oriented design and range of housing options served as the inspiration for the city's Downtown Livability Plan, passed in 2006. Despite ongoing financial and other challenges, the community continues to fight to sustain its viability. It serves as a reminder that it is not just a mix of buildings that define a place but, rather, the mix of people that infuses a neighborhood with a distinct voice and personality of its own.

Rachel the pig is the market's mascot and a piggy bank, collecting approximately $9,000 annually to support the social services provided by the market.

West Urbana, located between the University of
Illinois and downtown Urbana, has maintained a
distinct identity for more than a century. It is marked
by such treasures as Carle Park, which is home to
an arboretum, historic pavilion, and a Laredo Taft
sculpture of Abraham Lincoln, which stands
opposite the neighborhood high school.

Ryan Brault

CHAPTER 20

West Urbana
Urbana, Illinois

In West Urbana, it's not unusual to see scores of students walking to school while their parents walk or bike to work. The neighborhood's walkways, narrow streets, and picturesque shade trees and landscaping make traveling by foot desirable and contribute to a unique sense of place.

Located between two dynamic areas—the University of Illinois and downtown Urbana—West Urbana has maintained its neighborhood identity for more than a century, refusing to succumb to the pressures of high-density development or issues surrounding absentee landlords. Many historic properties remain today, the result of an active citizenry and sustained planning efforts.

A traditional residential neighborhood, West Urbana is best experienced on bike or foot. Nearly a quarter of commuters here don't use a car—about triple the national average. Children walk in groups to the local elementary school, an Art Deco-designed building from the 1930s federal Work Projects Administration (WPA). The high school and middle school also are within walking distance. The neighborhood has resisted the impulse to relocate its schools to larger locations on the edge of town, preferring instead to allow upgrades and some expansion.

West Urbana's physical design welcomes pedestrians. Twenty-three percent of employed residents commute to their jobs by walking, bicycling, or transit, compared to 8 percent nationwide.

The Urbana Free Library was founded in 1874 and was recently renovated and expanded. It has one of the highest usage rates in the nation. The Tortoise and Hare sculpture sits outside the door of the entrance to the children's library.

broken thoughts

West Urbana's physical design welcomes pedestrians. A discontinuous grid pattern, with T-intersections in key places to discourage cut-through vehicle traffic, provides connectivity and easy navigability. Mature trees form a canopy over narrow streets. Some roads and sidewalks feature restored brick. Historic, globe-style streetlamps and front porches combine to create an inviting streetscape for walkers, who often stop to chat with neighbors.

To promote additional bicycle and pedestrian use, the city is developing a bike master plan and, as streetscapes are updated, bike lanes and bump-outs are being constructed to improve safety and enhance accessibility. Twenty-three percent of employed residents commute to their jobs by walking, bicycling, or transit, compared to 8 percent nationwide.

Nonresidential features, such as the Urbana Free Library, also contribute to the neighborhood's strong sense of place. Founded in 1874 and recently renovated and expanded, the library has one of the highest usage rates in the nation. Another amenity, Carle Park, is home to an arboretum, historic pavilion, and a Laredo Taft sculpture of Abraham Lincoln.

From small, affordable homes to large, historic properties, houses in West Urbana are incredibly diverse and attract a wide cross-section of residents—traditional and single-parent families, couples, seniors, and individuals. Once viewed as a "faculty ghetto" due to its proximity to the university, the area is no longer dominated by a single employer.

Like many neighborhoods near college campuses, West Urbana faced demolitions and the replacement of single-family homes with student housing. As other historic neighborhoods to the north and west were lost to campus expansion

and other changes, West Urbana residents banded together in the early 1980s to convince city leaders to downzone the neighborhood in order to curtail similar development in their neighborhood.

The Downtown to Campus Plan, adopted in 1990, amended existing zoning to include "mixed office-residential" to promote adaptive reuse of older homes along Elm and Green Streets, and "campus commercial" to the north and west to provide an area where new student apartments would be allowed, relieving some development pressure in the neighborhood.

West Urbana offers a variety of housing styles and prices. Affordable small homes, well under $100,000, are found within the neighborhood as are large architect-designed homes that cost more than $500,000. Several of the

The tree canopy in West Urbana makes for some striking fall color displays.

Rob Olshansky

A conservation district ordinance would allow residential areas, which do not qualify for historic district status but that have unique qualities, to be protected by design review requirements.

West Urbana offers a variety of housing styles and prices. Affordable small homes, well under $100,000, are found within the neighborhood as are large architect-designed homes that cost more than $500,000.

neighborhood's homes have received local historic landmark designation including the Queen Anne style Lindley House and Ricker House, built in 1895 and 1892, respectively. Two other historic properties, built by Urbana architect Joseph Royer, include his personal residence—a Mission style home with an Arts and Crafts influence—and an English Revival style home for his mother-in-law.

Looking to the future, Urbana's 2005 Comprehensive Plan recommends creation of a West Urbana neighborhood conservation district and design guidelines for the Lincoln-Busey corridor. A conservation district ordinance would allow residential areas, which do not qualify for historic district status but that have unique qualities, to be protected by design review requirements. Neighborhood conservation district requirements would be enacted through an additional zoning overlay district that would supplement the underlying zoning requirements.

To make the neighborhood more sustainable, an ordinance was amended to promote the use of permeable pavement. Other amendments are being prepared to encourage the use of solar collectors and wind turbines.

After losing all of its magnificent elms to the Dutch elm disease in the 1950s and 1960s, Urbana planted thousands of new trees throughout the city, including West Urbana. As a result, the city received the first of its many Tree City USA designations in 1976.

Citizens have historically engaged in numerous planning activities to preserve the community's identity. Residents also have gotten involved through the local community association, which recently raised $12,500 to ensure that the city's

new street signs featured a historic design. The association has prepared white papers on issues of concern and sponsors a listserv to encourage discussion of neighborhood issues.

The association's website includes a calendar of events with a heavy emphasis on meetings and workshops targeted toward neighborhood planning and historic preservation. The group also sponsors events of its own such as a plant swap, house walk, neighborhood garage sale, seasonal clean-up, pot-luck afternoon in Carle Park, and at-large meetings.

Making a great neighborhood isn't always easy. But, as West Urbana shows, a sustainable community comes from involved residents willing to roll up their sleeves and plan for the future.

West Urbana's sidewalks and picturesque shade trees and landscaping make traveling by foot desirable and contribute to a unique sense of place.

MAKING GREAT COMMUNITIES HAPPEN

The American Planning Association provides leadership in the development of vital communities by advocating excellence in community planning, promoting education and citizen empowerment, and providing the tools and support necessary to effect positive change.

502. Parks and Economic Development. John L. Crompton. November 2001. 74pp.

503/504. Saving Face: How Corporate Franchise Design Can Respect Community Identity (revised edition). Ronald Lee Fleming. February 2002. 118pp.

505. Telecom Hotels: A Planners Guide. Jennifer Evans-Crowley. March 2002. 31pp.

506/507. Old Cities/Green Cities: Communities Transform Unmanaged Land. J. Blaine Bonham, Jr., Gerri Spilka, and Darl Rastorfer. March 2002. 123pp.

508. Performance Guarantees for Government Permit Granting Authorities. Wayne Feiden and Raymond Burby. July 2002. 80pp.

509. Street Vending: A Survey of Ideas and Lessons for Planners. Jennifer Ball. August 2002. 44pp.

510/511. Parking Standards. Edited by Michael Davidson and Fay Dolnick. November 2002. 181pp.

512. Smart Growth Audits. Jerry Weitz and Leora Susan Waldner. November 2002. 56pp.

513/514. Regional Approaches to Affordable Housing. Stuart Meck, Rebecca Retzlaff, and James Schwab. February 2003. 271pp.

515. Planning for Street Connectivity: Getting from Here to There. Susan Handy, Robert G. Paterson, and Kent Butler. May 2003. 95pp.

516. Jobs-Housing Balance. Jerry Weitz. November 2003. 41pp.

517. Community Indicators. Rhonda Phillips. December 2003. 46pp.

518/519. Ecological Riverfront Design. Betsy Otto, Kathleen McCormick, and Michael Leccese. March 2004. 177pp.

520. Urban Containment in the United States. Arthur C. Nelson and Casey J. Dawkins. March 2004. 130pp.

521/522. A Planners Dictionary. Edited by Michael Davidson and Fay Dolnick. April 2004. 460pp.

523/524. Crossroads, Hamlet, Village, Town (revised edition). Randall Arendt. April 2004. 142pp.

525. E-Government. Jennifer Evans-Cowley and Maria Manta Conroy. May 2004. 41pp.

526. Codifying New Urbanism. Congress for the New Urbanism. May 2004. 97pp.

527. Street Graphics and the Law. Daniel Mandelker with Andrew Bertucci and William Ewald. August 2004. 133pp.

528. Too Big, Boring, or Ugly: Planning and Design Tools to Combat Monotony, the Too-big House, and Teardowns. Lane Kendig. December 2004. 103pp.

529/530. Planning for Wildfires. James Schwab and Stuart Meck. February 2005. 126pp.

531. Planning for the Unexpected: Land-Use Development and Risk. Laurie Johnson, Laura Dwelley Samant, and Suzanne Frew. February 2005. 59pp.

532. Parking Cash Out. Donald C. Shoup. March 2005. 119pp.

533/534. Landslide Hazards and Planning. James C. Schwab, Paula L. Gori, and Sanjay Jeer, Project Editors. September 2005. 209pp.

535. The Four Supreme Court Land-Use Decisions of 2005: Separating Fact from Fiction. August 2005. 193pp.

536. Placemaking on a Budget: Improving Small Towns, Neighborhoods, and Downtowns Without Spending a Lot of Money. December 2005. 133pp.

537. Meeting the Big Box Challenge: Planning, Design, and Regulatory Strategies. Jennifer Evans–Crowley. March 2006. 69pp.

538. Project Rating/Recognition Programs for Supporting Smart Growth Forms of Development. Douglas R. Porter and Matthew R. Cuddy. May 2006. 51pp.

539/540. Integrating Planning and Public Health: Tools and Strategies To Create Healthy Places. Marya Morris, General Editor. August 2006. 144pp.

541. An Economic Development Toolbox: Strategies and Methods. Terry Moore, Stuart Meck, and James Ebenhoh. October 2006. 80pp.

542. Planning Issues for On-site and Decentralized Wastewater Treatment. Wayne M. Feiden and Eric S. Winkler. November 2006. 61pp.

543/544. Planning Active Communities. Marya Morris, General Editor. December 2006. 116pp.

545. Planned Unit Developments. Daniel R. Mandelker. March 2007.140pp.

546/547. The Land Use/Transportation Connection. Terry Moore and Paul Thorsnes, with Bruce Appleyard. June 2007. 440pp.

548. Zoning as a Barrier to Multifamily Housing Development. Garrett Knaap, Stuart Meck, Terry Moore, and Robert Parker. July 2007. 80pp.

549/550. Fair and Healthy Land Use: Environmental Justice and Planning. Craig Anthony Arnold. October 2007. 168pp.

552.. Great Places in America: Great Streets and Neighborhoods, 2007 Designees. April 2008. 84pp.

For price information, please go to APA's PlanningBooks.com or call 312-786-6344.
You will find a complete subject and chronological index to the PAS Report series at www.planning.org/pas.